LIVING IN STYLE
PARIS

LIVING IN STYLE
PARIS

Edited by Caroline Sarkozy
Photographs by Reto Guntli and Agi Simoes

teNeues

CONTENTS

Introduction

Depuis que le baron Haussmann a découpé à la hache le Paris de Balzac, où les bourgeois habitaient l'« étage noble » et les cousettes les mansardes du haut, Paris est devenu plus vaste et plus compartimenté. Capitale du raffinement et du romantisme, elle accueille en ses murs historiques des lieux rares et secrets. Ces endroits inédits sont autant de repères familiaux que de pied-à-terre d'étrangers amoureux de la ville.

Ce livre nous ouvre les portes d'univers exceptionnels où se côtoient splendeurs du XVIIIᵉ siècle, appartements haussmanniens et ateliers d'artistes.

Paris, trésor architectural, est le symbole de la culture française. Cette ville est le cœur vivant et palpitant de la France. Ses musées exceptionnels et ses monuments chargés d'histoire sont des joyaux. Il paraît normal que cette ville unique soit le berceau de tant de création. Nous retrouvons dans ces lieux très privilégiés les richesses du savoir-faire français : le travail d'artistes, d'artisans et de créateurs, qui excellent chacun dans sa spécialité.

Le charme de cette ville tient à sa population cosmopolite, classique et artistique. Le Parisien, plus qu'un dandy, est un mécène. Il aime l'art, l'élégance, la simplicité et le savoir-vivre. Discret, il apprécie d'inviter des convives de choix auxquels il souhaite faire partager le charme de son intérieur. Il aime l'élégance sophistiquée des splendeurs des siècles passés.

En feuilletant ce livre, vous découvrirez des appartements où l'art de vivre à la française a su associer traditionalisme et influences. Ces lieux confidentiels empreints de différentes cultures ont un magnétisme qui attire l'œil et éveille la curiosité. Nous avons aimé la sobriété, l'élégance simple, le raffinement discret, les tons apparemment neutres mais chauds, les objets choisis un par un, éclectiques dans leurs valeurs marchandes, dans leurs époques et dans leurs styles. Nos maîtres du goût sont, comme les femmes dont on est fou, « jamais ni tout à fait la même ni tout à fait une autre ». Ils ont, chacun à travers leurs goûts et leurs inspirations, donné à ces lieux une empreinte unique et singulière. Les collections d'œuvres d'art sont sublimées par ces mélanges d'étonnement et de raffinement.

Le lecteur se laissera emporter à la découverte de cette ville ou le terme décoration prend tout son sens.

Cette citation de Balzac me laisse rêveuse, mais elle décrit bien le sentiment que j'ai eu à travers mes pérégrinations dans ce Paris de la décoration : « Paris est un véritable océan. Jetez-y la sonde, vous n'en connaîtrez jamais la profondeur. Parcourez-le, décrivez-le : quelque soin que vous mettiez à le parcourir, à le décrire ; quelque nombreux et intéressés que soient les explorateurs de cette mer, il s'y rencontrera toujours un lieu vierge, un antre inconnu, des fleurs, des perles, des monstres, quelque chose d'inouï, oublié par les plongeurs littéraires. »

Caroline Sarkozy

Introduction

Since the time of Baron Haussmann's brutal reorganization of Balzac's Paris, where the bourgeois lived on the "noble floors" and the seamstresses occupied the attics, Paris has become vaster and more diversified. In this capital of refinement and romanticism, the historic walls of Paris hold many rare and secret dwellings. These unseen places are both family homes and *pieds-à-terre* owned by travelers in love with the city.

This book opens the doors to unique interiors where the splendors of the 18th century, Haussmannian apartments and artists' studios co-exist.

Paris, an architectural treasure, is the symbol of French culture. The city is the living, vibrant heart of France. Its unique museums and historical monuments are rare jewels. It seems fitting that this exceptional city should be the cradle to so much talent. We discover in these surprising homes the wealth of French creativity: the work of artists, artisans and designers, each excelling in their own realm.

The charm of the city comes from its cosmopolitan, classical and artistic population. The Parisian, more than a dandy, is a patron of the arts. He loves culture, elegance, simplicity and masters the elements of comfort. Discrete, he enjoys entertaining select visitors on whom he can bestow the generous charms of his French *savoir vivre,* and the sophisticated elegance of past centuries.

As you discover these pages, you will plunge into the French art of living where traditions and influences cross. These confidential residences, embalmed by multitudes of civilizations, have a magnetic quality that awakens one's curiosity and visual sense. I admired the sobriety, the simple elegance, the discrete refinement, the seemingly neutral but warm tones, the objects chosen one by one, eclectic in their market values, in their periods and finally in their style. Our masters of taste are, as the French poet Verlaine conveyed describing the flawless woman, "never completely the same, and never completely different." Each through their taste and inspiration, have created singular and spectacular refuges. The art collections are sublimated by their surprisingly eclectic nature and refined cohabitation.

The reader's enthusiasm will grow as he travels through this city where the term decoration finds its full meaning.

These words of Balzac leave me pensive. They describe with accuracy the sentiments I had as I ventured into this Paris of decoration: "Paris is an ocean. You may cast the sounding-line, but you will never fathom its depth. Walk through it, describe it: however painfully you explore it and sound its depths, however numerous and interested are the explorers of this ocean, there are still virgin corners, unknown caves, flowers, pearls, monsters, something unheard of, forgotten by literary divers."

Caroline Sarkozy

Einleitung

Seit Baron Haussmann das Paris von Balzac aufteilte, in dem das Bürgertum auf der „Beletage" wohnte und die Näherinnen unter dem Dach, hat es sich ausgedehnt und aufgefächert. Hinter dem historischen Gemäuer der Hauptstadt für Vornehmheit und Romantik, verbergen sich viele seltene und geheime Überraschungen. Diese unbemerkten Orte umfassen sowohl Häuser als auch kleine Wohnungen von Menschen, die die Stadt lieben und aus unterschiedlichen Ländern kommen.

Dieses Buch öffnet die Türen zu wunderbaren Universen, in denen die Pracht des 18. Jahrhunderts mit Wohnungen aus der Zeit von Haussmann und Künstlerateliers nebeneinander existieren.

Paris, ein architektonischer Schatz, steht für die französische Kultur. Die Stadt ist das lebendige, vibrierende Herz von Frankreich. Ihre einzigartigen Museen und geschichtsträchtigen Bauwerke stellen seltene Kostbarkeiten dar. Es erscheint ganz normal, dass diese Stadt eine solch schöpferische Wiege sein sollte. Wir entdecken an diesen sehr ungewöhnlichen Orten die Fülle französischen Know-hows: Werke von Künstlern, Kunsthandwerkern und Kreateuren, alle überragend in ihrem Fachgebiet.

Der Charme der Stadt liegt in ihrer kosmopolitischen, klassischen und künstlerischen Bevölkerung begründet. Der Pariser ist mehr als nur ein einfacher Dandy, er ist ein Mäzen der Künste. Er liebt die Kunst, Eleganz und Einfachheit. Und er weiß zu leben. Er lädt sich diskret besondere Gäste ein, mit denen er gemeinsam den Zauber seines Heims genießt. Er mag die vornehme Eleganz der vergangenen Jahrhunderte.

Beim Durchblättern dieser Seiten werden Sie Wohnungen entdecken, bei denen das französische Savoir-vivre den Traditionalismus mit verschiedensten Einflüssen verbindet. Diese geheimen Orte, geprägt durch verschiedene Kulturen, verfügen über eine besondere Anziehungskraft und erwecken unsere Neugierde. Wir waren begeistert von der Schlichtheit, der einfachen Eleganz, der diskreten Vornehmheit, der scheinbar neutralen, aber dennoch warmen Töne, der in Wert variierenden, aus verschiedenen Epochen und Stilen ausgewählten Objekte. Unsere Meister des Geschmacks schufen künstlerische Kreationen, die, wie die Frauen die man liebt, „nie vollständig gleich und nie vollständig anders" sind. Jeder von ihnen hat durch seinen Geschmack und seine Inspiration diesen Orten eine Einzigartigkeit und eine besondere Note verliehen. Die Kunstsammlungen werden durch diese Mischungen von Überraschung und Feinheit sublimiert.

Der Leser wird beim Entdecken dieser Stadt, bei der das Wort „Dekorieren" seine volle Bedeutung entfaltet, davongetragen.

Diese Worte von Balzac lassen mich ins Träumen geraten, doch beschreiben sie mein Gefühl auf meinen Streifzügen durch dieses Paris der Dekors: „Paris ist ein Meer. Man kann zwar einen Peilstock hineinwerfen, doch seine Tiefe wird man nie ausloten können. Spazieren Sie hindurch, beschreiben Sie es: Wie schmerzhaft die Entdeckungen und Tiefen, die Sie dabei ergründen werden und die Anzahl der interessierten Entdecker dieses Meeres auch sein mögen, es gibt immer noch unberührte Ecken, unbekannte Höhlen, Blumen, Perlen, Monster, etwas Ungehörtes, von den dichterischen Tauchern Vergessenes."

Caroline Sarkozy

Introducción

Desde que el barón Haussmann cortó a hachazos aquel París de Balzac en el que los burgueses habitaban la "planta noble" y las costureras vivían en las buhardillas, París ha pasado a ser más vasto y compartimentado. La ciudad, capital del refinamiento y el romanticismo, alberga entre sus históricos muros lugares singulares y secretos. Estos rincones ocultos los forman hogares familiares y pequeñas viviendas de extranjeros enamorados de la ciudad.

Este libro nos abre las puertas a universos extraordinarios donde los esplendores del siglo XVIII conviven con apartamentos haussmannianos y talleres de artistas.

París es un tesoro arquitectónico, símbolo de la cultura francesa. Esta ciudad es el corazón vivo y latente de Francia. Asimismo, sus excepcionales museos y sus monumentos, cargados de historia, son auténticas joyas. Por ello, resulta normal que esta ciudad única sea cuna de tanta creación. En estos rincones privilegiados descubrimos las riquezas de la maestría francesa; el trabajo de tantos artistas, artesanos y creadores, todos sobresalientes en su especialidad.

El encanto de esta ciudad nace de su población cosmopolita, clásica y artística. Más que un dandi, el parisino es un mecenas; siente amor por el arte, la elegancia, la simplicidad y el saber vivir. Es discreto y le gusta convidar a invitados especiales con los que desea compartir el encanto de su interior. Es amante de la elegancia sofisticada de los esplendores de siglos pasados.

Hojeando este libro descubrirá apartamentos en los que el arte de vivir a la francesa ha combinado con maestría tradicionalismo e influencias. Estos rincones secretos, impregnados de diferentes culturas, tienen un magnetismo especial que atrae la vista y despierta la curiosidad. En sus épocas y estilos, apreciamos la sobriedad, la elegancia sencilla, el refinamiento discreto, los tonos aparentemente neutros pero cálidos, los objetos escogidos uno a uno, eclécticos en su valor comercial. Nuestros maestros del gusto forjaron las creaciones artísticas, que, al igual que aquellas mujeres que adoramos, no son "nunca exactamente iguales ni completamente diferentes". A través de sus gustos e inspiraciones, cada uno de ellos ha otorgado a estos lugares un carácter único y singular. Así, las colecciones de arte se ven engrandecidas con estas mezclas de sorpresa y refinamiento.

El lector se dejará llevar al descubrimiento de esta ciudad, en la que el término decoración adquiere todo su sentido.

Estas palabras de Balzac despiertan a la soñadora que hay en mí, pero al mismo tiempo describen con fidelidad el sentimiento que me invadió en mis caminatas errantes por este París de la decoración: "París es un verdadero océano. Eche la sonda, pero nunca averiguará la profundidad. Recórralo, descríbalo; por mucho esmero que ponga en hacerlo, por muy numerosos y afanados que sean los exploradores de estas aguas, siempre se hallará un rincón virgen, una cueva desconocida, flores, perlas, monstruos, algo inaudito, olvidado por los buceadores literarios".

Caroline Sarkozy

Introduzione

Dall'epoca che vide il barone Haussmann stravolgere la Parigi di Balzac - la città della borghesia dei 'piani nobili' e delle umili sartine confinate tra le mura delle mansarde - la capitale francese ha assunto una fisionomia più estesa e compartimentata. Capitale della raffinatezza e del romanticismo, accoglie tra le sue mura intrise di storia luoghi inaspettati e reconditi, un bagaglio di spazi inediti, un corredo di abitazioni familiari così come di piccoli appartamenti acquistati da stranieri innamorati di questa città.

Questo libro ci introduce a uno straordinario universo in cui convivono fasti settecenteschi, appartamenti in stile Haussmann e atelier artistici.

Parigi, autentico prodigio architettonico, è l'emblema della cultura francese. Questa città rappresenta il nucleo incandescente, il cuore vivo e palpitante della Francia. I suoi straordinari musei e i monumenti carichi di storia sono capolavori unici. Non deve stupire dunque che una città senza pari come questa sia la culla di tanta energia creativa, un concentrato di luoghi eccezionali dove ci è dato ritrovare le immense ricchezze del gusto e della professionalità francesi: il lavoro di artisti, artigiani e inventori, ciascuno di essi un fuoriclasse del proprio ambito creativo.

Lo charme di questa città è frutto della natura cosmopolita, classica e artistica della sua popolazione. I parigini, più che semplici dandy, sono veri e propri mecenati. Amano l'arte, l'eleganza e la semplicità e conoscono bene le regole del buon vivere. Signorili e rispettosi, amano circondarsi di ospiti speciali con i quali condividere tutto il fascino dei propri spazi quotidiani. Apprezzano l'eleganza sofisticata dei fasti dei secoli passati.

Sfogliando le pagine di questo libro scoprirete appartamenti in cui l'arte di vivere francese ha saputo miscelare tradizionalismo e innovazione. Queste isole d'intimità recanti l'impronta di culture diverse possiedono un magnetismo che attira lo sguardo e risveglia la curiosità. Ne abbiamo apprezzato la sobrietà, l'eleganza essenziale, la signorile raffinatezza, i toni apparentemente neutri ma carichi di calore, gli oggetti scelti uno a uno in un eclettico carosello di epoche, stili e valori di mercato. I nostri maestri del gusto hanno forgiato creazioni artistiche che, come le donne che ci hanno conquistato il cuore, " non sono mai simili a sè stesse né mai completamente diverse ". Per mezzo del proprio stile e delle proprie ispirazioni, ciascuno di essi ha trasmesso a questi luoghi un'impronta unica e singolare, in un mélange di stupore e raffinatezza che ha trasformato le collezioni d'arte in un distillato di meraviglie.

Il lettore si lascerà condurre alla scoperta di una città in cui il concetto di decorazione si dispiega in tutti i suoi più intimi significati.

Questa formidabile citazione di Balzac descrive perfettamente i sentimenti che ho provato andando alla scoperta della Parigi della decorazione d'interni: " Parigi è un vero e proprio oceano. Per quanto possiate gettarvi la vostra sonda, non riuscirete mai a misurarne la profondità. Percorretela, raccontatela: quanto più impegno metterete nell'esplorarla fin dentro i suoi più reconditi recessi, tanto più numerosi e appassionati saranno coloro che si diranno pronti a scandagliare la vastità di un tale oceano, dove si incontreranno sempre una terra vergine, un antro sconosciuto, fiori, tesori, mostri sottomarini, qualcosa di sconosciuto, qualche insondabile profondità che gli esploratori convenzionali hanno dimenticato".

Caroline Sarkozy

Fashion Icon's Comeback

Saint-Germain-des-Prés

François Catroux and Diane von Furstenberg, close and longtime friends, set out to combine their shared sense of glamour and earthy simplicity to decorate her *pied-à-terre* in Paris. From her dining room window and as she sips her morning coffee, she can marvel over the view of the magnificent 17th-century Bibliothèque Mazarine, the oldest public library in France. Practical and comfort-oriented, they both aimed at creating a refined, timeless universe where her collection of original, ethnic chic fuses harmoniously with antiques and pieces by contemporary designers. A delicately painted Plexiglas coffee table designed by Kimoto Yoshida supports two rich fully colored porcelain birds, while an Andy Warhol portrait of Diane von Furstenberg hangs over a marble-top empire console and grooms the wall. As iconic as her jersey slinky wrap dresses, patterns and colors unravel and live on in her surroundings.

François Catroux et Diane von Fürstenberg, amis proches de longue date, ont entrepris de combiner leur goût commun pour la séduction et la simplicité naturelle en vue de décorer leur pied-à-terre à Paris. Depuis la fenêtre de la salle à manger, lorsqu'elle sirote son café le matin, Diane peut s'émerveiller à la vue de la magnifique bibliothèque Mazarine du XVIIᵉ siècle, la plus ancienne bibliothèque publique de France. Privilégiant l'aspect pratique et le confort, ils se sont tous deux attachés à créer un univers raffiné intemporel où la collection d'œuvres originales de diverses cultures se fond harmonieusement avec des œuvres anciennes et de designers contemporains. Sur une table basse en plexiglas subtilement décorée par Kimoto Yoshida paradent deux oiseaux de porcelaine bigarrés, alors qu'un portrait de Diane par Andy Warhol décore le mur auquel est adossée une console Empire à dessus en marbre. Comme son emblématique robe-portefeuille en jersey moulante, l'éclosion des motifs et couleurs donne au lieu un sens intemporel.

François Catroux und Diane von Fürstenberg, langjährige und enge Freunde mit Sinn für Glamour und irdische Schlichtheit, taten sich zusammen, um von Fürstenberg *pied-à-terre* in Paris einzurichten. Der Blick aus dem Esszimmer bietet morgens beim Frühstück den Blick auf die wundervolle Bibliothèque Mazarine, die älteste Leihbücherei Frankreichs, an der sie sich nicht sattsehen kann. Praktisches und Komfortables im Blick, setzten sich Catroux und von Fürstenberg das Ziel, ein raffiniertes und zeitloses Universum zu schaffen, in dem ihre Sammlung schicken und originellen Kunsthandwerks harmonisch mit zeitgenössischen Designerstücken und Antiquitäten verschmilzt. Über einen grazil bemalten Plexiglascouchtisch, ein Entwurf Kimoto Yoshidas, stolzieren zwei prächtige bunte Porzellanvögel, und ein Andy-Warhol-Porträt Diane von Fürstenbergs schmückt die Wand über einer Konsole mit Marmorplatte im Empire-Stil. Wie bei ihren ikonenhaften eng anliegenden Jersey-Wickelkleidern entfalten sich in ihrem Zuhause Muster und Farben.

François Catroux y Diane von Furstenberg, íntimos viejos amigos, se propusieron combinar el sentido del glamour y la poco sofisticada simplicidad que compartían para decorar su *pied-à-terre* en París. Desde la ventana del comedor y mientras sorbe su café matutino, puede deleitarse con las vistas de la magnífica Biblioteca Mazarino del siglo XVII, la biblioteca pública más antigua de Francia. Inclinados hacia la practicidad y la comodidad, ambos tenían como objetivo crear un universo refinado y atemporal en el que su colección de moda étnica original se fundiese armoniosamente tanto con piezas de diseñadores contemporáneos como con piezas antiguas. Una mesa de café de Plexiglas pintada con delicadeza y diseñada por Kimoto Yoshida sostiene dos pájaros de porcelana completamente coloreados con vivos colores, mientras un retrato de Diane von Furstenberg de Andy Warhol viste la pared que está se cierne sobre una consola con cubierta de mármol. Como su icónico vestido jersey ceñido, los motivos y los colores se desenredan y viven.

Forti di un'amicizia profonda, e di vecchia data, François Catroux e Diane von Furstenberg hanno concertato la vena glamour e la naturale semplicità che li accomuna per decorare il *pied-à-terre* parigino di Diane. Dalla finestra della sala da pranzo, davanti al primo caffè del mattino, Diane può contemplare la splendida mole seicentesca della Bibliothèque Mazarine, la più antica biblioteca pubblica di Francia. Animati da uno spiccato senso pratico che li orienta verso la ricerca del comfort, hanno lavorato per creare un raffinato universo sospeso nel tempo in cui la collezione di eleganti pezzi etnici originali della padrona di casa si fondesse armoniosamente con gli elementi di design contemporaneo e i pezzi d'epoca. Su un tavolino in Plexiglas dai delicati decori disegnato da Kimoto Yoshida poggiano due vivaci uccelli in porcellana dai colori saturi, mentre il ritratto di Diane von Furstenberg opera di Andy Warhol domina la parete sopra una consolle in marmo stile Impero. Così come l'inconfondibile e seducente abito in jersey che fascia Diane, motivi e colori si affermano e diventano eterni.

A Wengé bookshelf lines the walls of her library and is filled with personal mementos, family photos and an Andy Warhol portrait of Marilyn Monroe. A cast iron bed from the Restoration period is upholstered with rich colored silk. An interesting rocking chair made out of the metal used for taxiways in African rural airports during the colonial era sits in a corner. The zebra patterned carpet is a Diane von Furstenberg design and creation. The guest room has no doors but there is a beautifully crafted folding screen in green silk fabric lined with antique nails. A mahogany art deco desk with golden sock legs stands in front of the guest room, with an orange ceramic lamp designed in 1910.

Dans les rayons en bois de wengé qui couvrent les murs de sa bibliothèque, on peut voir des souvenirs personnels, des photos de famille et un portrait de Marilyn Monroe par Andy Warhol. Un lit en fonte Restauration est rembourré de soie aux couleurs chaudes. Une intéressante chaise à bascule façonnée dans le métal utilisé pour les voies de circulation dans les aéroports d'Afrique rurale durant l'ère coloniale trône dans un coin. Le tapis à motif zébré est une création de Diane von Fürstenberg. Pas de porte pour accéder à la chambre d'amis, mais un paravent magnifiquement ouvragé, tendu de tissu de soie verte à l'aide de vieux clous. Sur le bureau Art déco en acajou à pieds chemisés d'or installé dans l'ouverture donnant sur la chambre d'amis est posée une lampe de table en céramique orange de 1910.

Bücherregale aus Wengé überziehen die Wände ihrer Bibliothek und sind mit persönlichen Erinnerungsstücken, Familienfotos und einem Andy-Warhol-Porträt Marilyn Monroes bestückt. Mit prächtiger bunter Seide wurde ein gusseisernes Bett aus der Zeit der Restauration aufgepolstert. In einer Ecke steht ein interessanter Schaukelstuhl, der aus Metall konstruiert wurde, das während der Kolonialzeit für die Rollbahnen der afrikanischen Flughäfen auf dem Lande diente. Der Teppich mit Zebramuster wurde von Diane von Fürstenberg entworfen und gefertigt. Das Gästezimmer hat keine Türen, sondern einen wunderbar gearbeiteten Paravent aus grüner Seide, der mit antiken Nägeln beschlagen ist. Ein Art-déco-Tisch aus Mahagoni mit vergoldeten Tischbeinen und einer orangefarbenen Keramiklampe von 1910 steht im Eingang zum Gästezimmer.

Un estante de acabado wengué cubre las paredes de la librería y está repleto de recuerdos personales, fotos familiares y un retrato de Marilyn Monroe de Andy Warhol. Una cama de hierro fundido del periodo de la Restauración está tapizada con seda de vivos colores. En un rincón se halla una interesante mecedora hecha del metal usado para calles de rodaje en aeropuertos rurales africanos durante la época colonial. La moqueta cebrada esta diseñada y creada por Diane von Furstenberg. El cuarto de invitados no tiene puertas, sino un precioso biombo de tela de seda verde, adornado con antiguos clavos. Un escritorio art déco de caoba con patas doradas se encuentra frente al cuarto de invitados, con una lámpara de cerámica naranja diseñada en el año 1910.

Una scaffalatura in wengè riveste le pareti della biblioteca animata da ricordi personali, foto di famiglia e dai colori vividi di un ritratto di Marilyn Monroe di Andy Warhol. Il letto Restaurazione in ferro è rivestito con tessuto in seta dalle tonalità intense. In un angolo fa capolino un'interessante sedia a dondolo realizzata con il metallo usato per le taxiway negli aeroporti rurali africani in epoca coloniale. Il tappeto zebrato è una creazione personale di Diane von Furstenberg. Alla camera degli ospiti, che non ha porte tradizionali, dà accesso un insieme di ante a soffietto di splendida fattura con rivestimento in seta verde bordato di chiodi antichi. Di fronte, una scrivania in mogano art déco con gambaletto dorato sorregge una lampada in ceramica arancio del 1910.

The living room displays a cozy silk sofa in golden beige by Catroux, two copper-toned pouf styled coffee tables by Hervé Van Der Straeten flanked by two African crafted armchairs confectioned in colored pearl beads. Richard Avedon photos, sofa and cushions designed by Catroux, and another Van Der Straeten pouf style coffee table create a refined comfortable space.

Dans le salon nous accueillent un sofa bien douillet en soie beige doré de Catroux, deux tables basses style pouf dessinées par Hervé Van Der Straeten, flanquées de deux fauteuils africains réalisés à partir de perles véritables. Des photos de Richard Avedon, un canapé et des coussins dessinés par Catroux et une autre table basse de style pouf de Van Der Straeten créent une atmosphère raffinée et confortable.

Im Wohnzimmer prunken ein einladendes gold-beiges Seidensofa von Catroux und zwei kupferfarbene Beistelltische von Hervé Van der Straeten, die von zwei in Handarbeit mit bunten Perlen besetzten afrikanischen Sesseln flankiert werden. Mit Fotos von Richard Avedon, einem Sofa und Kissen von Catroux sowie einem weiteren Beistelltisch von Van der Straeten entsteht ein edler und zugleich behaglicher Raum.

En el salón se encuentra un cómodo sofá de seda en tono beige dorado de Catroux, dos mesitas de café de estilo puf en tonos cobrizos de Hervé Van Der Straeten flanqueadas por dos sillones de artesanía africana confeccionados con abalorios de perla coloreados. Fotos de Richard Avedon, sofá y cojines diseñados por Catroux y otra mesita de café en estilo puf de Van Der Straeten para crear un espacio cómodo y refinado.

Nel living, davanti al morbido sofà di Catroux rivestito in seta beige dorata, due coffee-table stile pouf con finitura rame di Hervé Van Der Straeten si frappongono a una coppia di poltroncine artigianali africane tempestate di perle colorate. Ritratti di Richard Avedon, un sofà con cuscini disegnato da Catroux e un altro coffee-table stile pouf di Van Der Straeten danno vita a uno spazio raffinato e confortevole.

Napoleon Spirit

Jardin des Tuileries

Driven by a passion for history, it took this American collector in Paris years and a strong sense of perfection to create a *pied-à-terre* fit for Napoleon Bonaparte himself. He set out on a quest to revive the neoclassic aesthetics of the Empire style, and every detail celebrates this period and the illustrious character that famed it. The dining room displays an 18th-century Venetian blown glass chandelier, frescos by Dufour on the story of Psyche, Consulat period chairs, and a porcelain service that once belonged to Joséphine. One side of the sumptuous living room has a Directoire pedestal table, a blue marble mantelpiece with terracotta eagle-headed lions flanked by one of Napoleon's throne style office chairs designed by Jacob Frères. The entrance hallway is paved with three-tone 18th-century marble, 2nd-century Roman torches, busts of Socrates and Homer, 1st-century Roman marble fragments and relics—each and every detail deepens the sense of power and pays tribute to the Empire's place in history.

Mû par sa passion de l'Histoire, ce collectionneur américain vivant à Paris a eu besoin de plusieurs années et d'un grand esprit de perfectionnisme pour réaliser un pied-à-terre qui puisse convenir à Napoléon Bonaparte en personne. Il s'est résolu à faire revivre l'esthétique néoclassique du style Empire, et chaque détail glorifie cette période et l'illustre personnage qui a fait sa renommée. Dans la salle à manger, on peut admirer un lustre XVIIIe en verre vénitien soufflé, des fresques de Dufour retraçant la vie de Psyché, des chaises Consulat et un service en porcelaine ayant jadis appartenu à Joséphine. L'une des extrémités de la somptueuse salle à manger est ornée d'un guéridon Directoire, d'un manteau de cheminée de marbre bleu soutenu par des lions en terre cuite à tête d'aigle et d'un fauteuil de bureau Napoléon en forme de trône et dessiné par Jacob Frères. Dans le vestibule de l'entrée, des dalles de marbre du XVIIIe en trois teintes, des torches romaines du IIe siècle, des bustes de Socrate et d'Homère, des vestiges et reliques romans du Ier siècle : il n'est pas un détail qui n'accentue le sentiment de puissance et ne rende hommage à la place de l'Empire dans l'Histoire.

Angetrieben von seiner Passion für Geschichte musste dieser in Paris lebende Amerikaner und Sammler mehrere Jahre und viel Perfektionismus aufbringen, um dieses *pied-à-terre* einzurichten, in dem sich auch Napoleon Bonaparte selbst wohlfühlen würde. Er war bestrebt, die neoklassische Ästhetik des Kaiserreichs wiederaufleben zu lassen, und jedes Detail preist diese Epoche und den illustren Charakter, durch den sie berühmt wurde. Das Esszimmer ist mit einem venezianischen Glaslüster aus dem 18. Jahrhundert, Wandbildern von Dufour, die die Geschichte der Psyche darstellen, Stühlen aus der Zeit des französischen Konsulats und Porzellan, das einst Kaiserin Joséphine gehörte, ausgestattet. Auf der einen Seite des Esszimmers steht ein Directoire-Säulentisch vor einem Kaminsims aus blauem Marmor mit Terrakotta-Greifen und daneben einer von Napoleons thronartigen Bürosesseln, ein Entwurf von Jacob Frères. Marmor des 18. Jahrhunderts in drei Farbtönen wurde in der Eingangshalle ausgelegt, die mit römischen Leuchtern aus dem 2. Jahrhundert, Büsten von Sokrates und Homer sowie Marmorreliquien und -fragmenten aus dem 1. Jahrhundert geschmückt ist. Jedes einzelne Detail verstärkt den Eindruck der Macht und zollt dem Platz, den das Kaiserreich in der Geschichte einnimmt, Tribut.

Impulsado por la pasión por la historia, este estadounidense afincado en París y coleccionista necesitó años y un fuerte sentido de la perfección para crear un *pied-à-terre* adecuado para el proprio Napoleón Bonaparte. Se dispuso para una búsqueda para revivir la estética neoclásica del estilo imperial y cada detalle celebra este periodo y el ilustre carácter que lo hizo famoso. El comedor presenta una lámpara de araña de cristal veneciano soplado del siglo XVIII, frescos de Dufour sobre la historia de Psique, sillas del periodo Consulat y un servicio de porcelana que una vez perteneció a Joséphine. Un lado del suntuoso salón alberga una mesa de pedestal Directoire, una repisa de chimenea de mármol azul con leones de terracota que tienen cabezas de águila, flanqueados por una de las sillas de oficina estilo trono de Napoleón, diseñada por Jacob Frères. El vestíbulo de entrada está pavimentado con tres tonalidades de mármol del siglo XVIII, antorchas romanas del siglo II, bustos de Sócrates y Homero y fragmentos y reliquias romanas de mármol del siglo I. Todos y cada uno de los detalles profundizan en el sentimiento de poder y rinden tributo al lugar que el Imperio ocupa en la historia.

Animato da un'autentica passione per la storia, questo collezionista americano di stanza a Parigi ha impiegato anni e affinato una spiccata inclinazione alla perfezione per forgiare un *pied-à-terre* degno del Napoleone Bonaparte che dimora in lui. Aspirando a rinfocolare l'estetica neoclassica dello stile Impero, la ricerca intrapresa dal proprietario esalta ogni dettaglio di questo periodo artistico e il personaggio illustre che lo rese famoso. Nella sala da pranzo primeggia un lampadario veneziano in vetro soffiato del XVIII secolo, tra affreschi di Dufour sulla storia di Psiche, poltroncine in stile Consolato e un servizio di porcellane appartenuto a Joséphine. Danno risalto a un lato del sontuoso living un tavolino con piedistallo in stile Directoire, un camino in marmo azzurro cinto da leoni con testa d'aquila in terracotta e, a fianco, una delle poltroncine-scranno di Napoleone opera di Jacob Frères. Tre tonalità di marmo settecentesco pavimentano il corridoio d'ingresso, cui fanno da cornice torce romane del II secolo, busti di Socrate e Omero, frammenti di marmi e reperti romani del I secolo, con ogni minimo dettaglio teso ad accentuare la suggestione del potere e a rendere omaggio al ruolo dell'Impero nella storia.

Opposite to the mantelpiece, this view of the living room displays paintings by Augustin-Louis Belle, 1793 depicting the encounter of Theseus with his son and a portrait of the Countess Mollien by Robert Lefèvre from 1806. Consulat style cabinets flank the entrance to the study and two Empire armchairs sit by a bust of Casimir Delavigne signed David d'Angers.

Cette vue de la salle de sejour à l'opposé du manteau de cheminée permet d'admirer deux tableaux, l'un de 1793 par Augustin-Louis Belle qui illustre la rencontre de Thésée avec son fils, et l'autre, de 1806, dans lequel Robert Lefèvre dresse le portrait de la comtesse Mollien. Deux petites commodes Consulat flanquent l'entrée du bureau et deux fauteuils Empire font face à un buste de David d'Angers représentant Casimir Delavigne.

Im Wohnzimmer hängen gegenüber dem Kamin große Gemälde; eines von Augustin-Louis Belle von 1793, das die Begegnung Theseus' mit seinem Sohn darstellt, sowie ein Porträt der Gräfin Mollien von Robert Lefèvre von 1806. Schränke im Konsulat-Stil flankieren den Eingang zum Arbeitszimmer und zwei Sessel im Empire-Stil stehen neben einer Büste Casimir Delavignes von David d'Angers.

Frente a la repisa de la chimenea, esta vista del salón muestra pinturas de Augustin-Louis Belle que representan el encuentro de Teseo con su hijo (1793), así como un retrato de la Condesa Mollien de Robert Lefèvre en 1806. Gabinetes en estilo Consulat flanquean la entrada del estudio y dos butacas imperiales yacen junto a un busto de Casimir Delavigne firmado por David d'Angers.

Opposta al camino, questa prospettiva del living rivela dipinti di Augustin-Louis Belle, tra cui uno del 1793 raffigurante l'incontro tra Teseo e il figlio, e un ritratto della contessa Mollien realizzato da Robert Lefèvre nel 1806. Credenze stile Consolato presidiano l'ingresso dello studio, con due poltrone stile Impero accanto a un busto di Casimir Delavigne firmato David d'Angers.

Carpenter's Workshop
Bastille

When Hervé Van Der Straeten first saw this 19th-century workshop, he imagined traveling through time to make a revival of decorative protagonists of each period. He removed walls and opened spaces; with white raw concrete stainless steel lined floors and pure superfluous toned walls, he raises the curtain, staging distinct objects that delight in an open dialogue where baroque meets modernism and pieces of contemporary art oppose five-legged Louis XV chairs. He brings them all back to life with a fresh new look, re-upholstering the traditional black leather Le Corbusier armchairs with emerald green satin, placing a 17th-century gold-gilded mirror on a polished stainless steel mirror console that he designed. An imposing orange giant by Xavier Veilhan guards the living room. With no doors, each space opens to an entirely different set. The cherry red of the velvet curtains spills and splashes in the bedroom. Under the spotlight, each piece plays their part, with an understanding that it is their strong personalities that pulls them all together.

Lorsqu'il découvre cet atelier du XIXe siècle, Hervé Van Der Straeten imagine un voyage à travers le temps afin de faire revivre les artistes qui l'ont occupé à diverses époques. Il supprime des cloisons et ouvre les espaces avec des dalles blanches en béton brut bordé d'acier inox et des murs également aux tons purs. Là, il met en scène des objets qui se plaisent à dialoguer librement, le baroque côtoyant le moderne et les œuvres contemporaines s'opposant aux chaises Louis XV à cinq pieds. Il les fait revivre grâce à un nouvel éclairage : il retend ainsi de satin vert les fauteuils Le Corbusier habituellement en cuir noir et place un miroir du XVIIe siècle à cadre doré sur une console miroir de sa conception en acier inox poli. Un impressionnant géant orange de Xavier Veilhan monte la garde dans le salon. Les espaces dénués de portes ouvrent tous sur un décor totalement différent. Les rideaux en velours répandent leur rouge cerise, qui éclabousse la chambre. Chaque objet mis en scène joue son rôle, conscient de ce que la forte personnalité de chacun d'entre eux les rassemble.

Als Hervé Van Der Straeten die Räume dieser Manufaktur aus dem 19. Jahrhundert das erste Mal sah, stellte er sich gleich eine Zeitreise vor, in der die Protagonisten der Dekoration aus verschiedenen Epochen ein Revival erleben. Er riss Wände heraus und erweiterte die Räume mit ihren weißen, von Edelstahllinien eingefassten Rohbetonböden und farbigen Wandscheiben. Er schafft eine Bühne und inszeniert Objekte, die in einem offenen Dialog übersprudeln, wo das Barock auf die Moderne trifft und Werke zeitgenössischer Kunst fünfbeinigen Louis-quinze-Stühlen gegenüberstehen. Er haucht ihnen mit einem frischen, neuartigen Look neues Leben ein, beispielsweise wenn er die traditionell schwarzen Ledersessel Le Corbusiers mit smaragdgrünem Satin bezieht oder einen vergoldeten Spiegel aus dem 17. Jahrhundert auf eine selbstentworfene spiegelnde Edelstahlkonsole stellt. Ein stattlicher orangefarbener Riese von Xavier Veilhan wacht über den Wohnraum. Türenlos öffnet sich jeder Raum zu einem ganz anderen Szenenaufbau. Das Kirschrot der Samtgardinen scheint überzulaufen und hat sich im gesamten Schlafzimmer verbreitet. So ins Rampenlicht gerückt, spielen die einzelnen Elemente ihre eigene Rolle, ergeben aber dank ihrer starken Persönlichkeiten gleichzeitig ein konsistentes Gesamtbild.

Cuando Hervé Van Der Straeten vio por primera vez este taller del siglo XIX, se imaginó viajando en el tiempo para lograr el renacimiento de los protagonistas decorativos de cada periodo. Retiró paredes y abrió espacios, con suelos blancos de hormigón en bruto surcados por líneas de acero inoxidable y paredes de tonos puros superfluos, levantó el telón para poner en escena diferentes objetos que se regocijan en un diálogo abierto donde el barroco y el modernismo se dan la mano y las piezas de arte contemporáneo contrastan con sillas Luis XV de cinco patas. Él los trae a todos de regreso a la vida con un look fresco renovado, tapizando de nuevo los tradicionales sillones Le Corbusier de cuero negro con seda verde esmeralda, colocando un espejo dorado del siglo XVII en una consola de espejo de acero inoxidable pulido diseñada por él mismo. Un imponente gigante naranja de Xavier Veilhan custodia el salón. Cada espacio carece de puertas y se abre a un escenario completamente distinto. El rojo cereza de las cortinas de terciopelo se derrama y salpica el dormitorio. Bajo los focos, cada pieza desempeña su papel, conscientes de que son sus fuertes personalidades las que las unen.

La prima volta che Hervé Van Der Straeten ha visto questo vecchio laboratorio del XIX secolo ha immaginato di poter viaggiare sulle ali del tempo per far rivivere i protagonisti dell'arte decorativa di ogni epoca. Ha eliminato pareti e allargato gli spazi, rivestendoli di pavimenti bianchi in cemento grezzo con finiture in acciaio e pareti dalle tonalità adamantine, ha utilizzato tendaggi che come sipari si aprono su un insieme di oggetti dissimili uniti in un dialogo gioioso e dinamico in cui il barocco incontra il modernismo e l'arte contemporanea fa da contrappunto a sedie Luigi XV a cinque gambe. Van Der Straeten riporta in auge ciascuno di questi elementi con tratti freschi e aggiornati, sostituendo la pelle nera delle tradizionali poltrone Le Corbusier con il satin verde smeraldo e collocando uno specchio del XVII secolo con finitura in lamina d'oro sopra una consolle in acciaio lucido da lui stesso disegnata. Un imperioso Gigante arancio di Xavier Veilhan fa da sentinella alla zona living. Privi di porte, gli spazi si aprono ciascuno su ambienti del tutto dissimili. Il rosso ciliegia delle tende in velluto trabocca nella camera da letto fino a inondarla. Rivestito dalla luce ciascun elemento assume un ruolo ben definito, con la consapevolezza della propria spiccata personalità quale elemento di raccordo che crea unità.

In the dining room, a 17th-century Spanish gold-gilded mirror rests on a Hervé Van Der Straeten polished stainless steel "Piercing" console. The bi-color lacquered wood dining room table is also one of his designs. A bombastic black planetary mobile designed by Xavier Veilhan inhabits the opposite side of the dining room.

Dans la salle à manger, un miroir espagnol du XVIIe siècle à cadre doré repose sur la console « piercing » en acier inox poli imaginée par Hervé Van Der Straeten. La table en bois laqué bicolore est également l'une de ses créations. Un imposant mobile de planètes noires signé Xavier Veilhan occupe l'autre extrémité de la salle à manger.

Ein vergoldeter spanischer Spiegel aus dem 17. Jahrhundert ruht auf einer glänzenden Edelstahlkonsole von Hervé Van Der Straeten. Der zweifarbige Lack-Esstisch ist ebenfalls einer seiner Entwürfe. Ein bombastisches schwarzes Planeten-Mobile von Xavier Veilhan fängt die Blicke auf der gegenüberliegenden Seite des Esszimmers ein.

En el comedor, un espejo español dorado del siglo XVII reposa en una consola "piercing" de acero inoxidable pulido de Hervé Van Der Straeten. La mesa del comedor de madera de lacado bicolor es también uno de sus diseños. Un bombástico planetario móvil negro diseñado por Xavier Veilhan habita la parte opuesta del comedor.

Nella sala da pranzo, uno specchio spagnolo in lamina d'oro del XVII secolo s'impone sulla consolle "Piercing" in acciaio lucido disegnata da Hervé Van Der Straeten, che ha firmato anche il tavolo da pranzo bicromo in legno laccato. Un iperbolico mobile planetario nero di Xavier Veilhan crea un dinamico insieme sul lato opposto della stanza.

Hollywood Revisited

Palais-Bourbon

When you enter this exquisite apartment, it is like stepping into a Hollywood set at the peak of its Golden Age. Each and every detail exudes the ultimate glamour incarnate of Marlene Dietrich, Greta Garbo and Joan Crawford. Pierre Passebon wanted to create a setting that resembles its owner: elegant, modern and agelessly beautiful. Structural changes were made to build monumental columns and geometric style parquetry. The entrance's all-in-white wall has horizontal friezes, geometric fretwork moldings, and it features a marble top console by Gilbert Poillerat flanked by 1930s Medusa wall lamps by Diego Giacometti and a Bauhaus chandelier that once belonged to John Lennon. On one side of the living room, a 1940s Murano mirror hangs above an early 19th-century neoclassic bronze signed Bertel Thorvaldsen set on a fireplace by André Arbus. A pair of green and yellow chairs by Jacques Quinet stand in front a coffee table designed by Marc du Plantier in the 1930s. It is the fusion of contemporary art and photographs that snap us back to the 21st century.

En entrant dans ce délicieux appartement, on a l'impression de pénétrer dans un décor de l'âge d'or d'Hollywood. Des moindres détails rayonne l'absolue fascination incarnée par Marlene Dietrich, Greta Garbo et Joan Crawford. Pierre Passebon a souhaité créer un cadre qui ressemble à sa propriétaire : élégant, moderne et d'une beauté intemporelle. Il a modifié la structure du lieu, afin d'introduire de monumentales colonnes et un parquet à motifs géométriques. Les murs blanc uni de l'entrée, sur lesquels sont plaqués des appliques méduses 1930 de Diego Giacometti et un lustre Bauhaus ayant appartenu à John Lennon, sont rehaussés de frises horizontales, de corniches à formes géométriques et d'une console à dessus en marbre de Gilbert Poillerat. D'un côté du salon, un miroir Murano 1940 pend au-dessus d'un bronze néoclassique XIXe de Bertel Thorvaldsen, reposant sur une cheminée d'André Arbus. Deux chaises vert et jaune de Jacques Quinet font face à une table basse 1930 de Marc du Plantier. Enfin, le mariage entre l'art contemporain et les photographies nous fait revenir au XXIe siècle.

Diese großartige Wohnung zu betreten, ist wie ein Hollywood-Filmstudio zu seinen Glanzzeiten zu besuchen. Jedes einzelne Detail verströmt den einzigartigen Glamour, wie ihn Marlene Dietrich, Greta Garbo und Joan Crawford verkörperten. Pierre Passebon wollte eine Einrichtung schaffen, die der Wohnungseigentümerin entspricht: elegant, modern und zeitlos schön. Nach baulichen Anpassungen konnten gewaltige Säulen und Parkettböden mit geometrischen Mustern eingebaut werden. Im ganz in Weiß gehaltenen Eingangsbereich mit horizontalen Friesen und geometrischen Holzschnitzereien steht ein Tisch mit Marmorplatte von Gilbert Poillerat, umgeben von 1930er Medusen-Wandleuchten von Diego Giacometti und einem Bauhauslüster, der einst John Lennon gehörte. An der Seite des Wohnzimmers hängt ein Murano-Spiegel aus den 1940er Jahren über einer klassizistischen Bronze von Bertel Thorvaldsen aus dem frühen 19. Jahrhundert, die auf einem Kamin von André Arbus steht. Zwei grün-gelbe Sessel von Jacques Quinet stehen neben einem Couchtisch, der in den 1930er Jahren von Marc du Plantier entworfen wurde. Die Verquickung mit zeitgenössischer Kunst und Fotografien holt den Betrachter zurück in das 21. Jahrhundert.

Entrar en este exquisito apartamento es como poner los pies en un plató de Holywood en el cénit de su edad de oro. Cada detalle irradia la encarnación del glamour más sofisticado de Marlene Dietrich, Greta Garbo y Joan Crawford. Pierre Passebon deseaba crear un entorno semejante a su dueño: elegante, moderno y de eterna belleza. Se realizaron cambios estructurales para construir columnas monumentales y parqué en estilo geométrico. El muro completamente blanco de la entrada cuenta con frisos horizontales así como molduras de calado geométricas y presenta una consola con parte superior de mármol de Gilbert Poillerat, acompañada por lámparas de pared de los años 30 con forma de cabeza de medusa por Diego Giacometti y una araña de luces de Bauhaus que una vez perteneció a John Lennon. En un lado del salón, un espejo de Murano de los años 40 pende sobre un bronce neoclásico de principios del siglo XIX firmado por Bertel Thorvaldsen, colocado a su vez sobre una chimenea de André Arbus. Un par de sillas verdes y amarillas de Jacques Quinet se sitúan frente a una mesa de café diseñada por Marc du Plantier en los años 30. Son la fusión del arte contemporáneo y las fotografías lo que nos devuelve al siglo XXI.

Entrare in questo delizioso appartamento è come aprire la porta di un set cinematografico dell'epoca d'oro hollywoodiana. Da ogni minimo particolare stilla tutto il fascino di inarrivabili divine, come Marlene Dietrich, Greta Garbo e Joan Crawford. Pierre Passebon ha voluto creare un ambiente che assomigliasse al suo proprietario: elegante, moderno e di una bellezza senza tempo. Alcune modifiche strutturali hanno consentito la realizzazione delle colonne classiche e del parquet a motivi geometrici. Sulla bianca parete dell'ingresso, scandita da scanalature orizzontali con modanatura dentellata a motivi geometrici, risaltano una console con piano in marmo di Gilbert Poillerat, lampade a muro a testa di Medusa degli anni '30 di Diego Giacometti e un lampadario Bauhaus, un tempo appartenuto a John Lennon. Su una parete del living, uno specchio di Murano anni '40 scende sopra un bronzo neoclassico di inizio del XIX secolo di Bertel Thorvaldsen appoggiato su un caminetto di André Arbus. Una coppia di sedie verdi e gialle di Jacques Quinet completa il tavolino disegnato da Marc du Plantier negli anni '30. L'alternarsi di fotografie e arte contemporanea è l'elemento che ci riporta all'attualità del XXI secolo.

The bathroom features a golden marble top sink and a Venetian chandelier by Veronese. In the bedroom, André Arbus designed the faux leopard fur covered bed in the 1930s, and Helmut Newton and Robert Mapplethorpe photos hang above an art deco console.

Dans la salle de bains, un chandelier vénitien de Véronèse surplombe un lavabo à dessus en marbre doré. Dans la chambre, le lit 1930 dessiné par André Arbus est recouvert d'une fourrure imitation léopard. Des photos de Helmut Newton et Robert Mapplethorpe sont accrochées au-dessus d'une console Art déco.

Das Badezimmer ist mit einem goldenen Marmorwaschtisch und einem venezianischen Leuchter von Veronese ausgestattet. Das Bett mit einem Überwurf aus nachgemachten Leopardenfellen entwarf André Arbus in den 1930er Jahren, und über einer Art déco-Konsole hängen Fotos von Helmut Newton und Robert Mapplethorpe.

El baño presenta un lavabo de mármol dorado y una araña de luces veneciana de Veronese. En el dormitorio, la cama cubierta con pieles de imitación de leopardo diseñada por André Arbus en los años 30 y fotos de Helmut Newton y Robert Mapplethorpe que cuelgan sobre una consola art déco.

Nel bagno risaltano il lavandino con top in marmo e il lampadario veneziano di Veronese. Nella camera padronale, il letto anni '30 di André Arbus con copriletto in finta pelliccia di leopardo è completato da ritratti di Helmut Newton e Robert Mapplethorpe appesi sopra una console art déco.

Forever Chic

Élysée

Situated in the most exclusive area of Paris, known as the "Golden Triangle," this *pied-à-terre* could be an image from the Roaring Twenties in all its decadence. Based on pure architectural lines, Laurent Bourgois and home interiors company CS décoration combined forces to fulfill their client's desires. With this luxuriously simple setting, they have successfully combined works of contemporary art with exceptional 20th-century furniture using humor and grace. Each object in the collection is honored: whether it be the sobriety of the painting, the selection of the marble, the careful crafting of the woodwork, or the meticulous search for carpets and fabrics. The magnificent painting *Stardust Memories* by Christoph Ruckhäberle appears to hover over the comfortable cream couch. The simplistic Barcelona coffee table by Mies van der Rohe, is offset by the red, 1960s armchairs by Maxime Old and the indigo stools by Michel Boyer (made in 1968).

Situé dans le très chic quartier de Paris surnommé le Triangle d'or, ce pied-à-terre pourrait être à l'image des Années folles et de leur décadence. S'appuyant sur des lignes architecturales pures, Laurent Bourgois, architecte, et CS décoration ont trouvé dans leur collaboration une réponse aux attentes de leur client. Dans cet écrin luxueux et sobre, ils ont réussi avec humour et élégance à associer à des œuvres d'art contemporaines du mobilier d'exception du XXᵉ siècle. La sobriété des laques, la sélection des marbres, le traitement soigné des menuiseries, la recherche pointue de tapis et tissus rendent hommage à tous ces objets de collection. L'immense « Stardust Memories » de Christoph Ruckhäberle semble se renverser sur le confortable canapé blanc crème. La sobriété de la table basse « Barcelona » de Mies van der Rohe tranche avec le rouge des fauteuils 1960 de Maxime Old et le bleu indigo des tabourets de Michel Boyer (créés en 1968).

Diese Wohnung liegt in einem sehr schicken Teil von Paris, der *le tringle d'or* genannt wird, und erinnert an den Glamour und die Dekadenz der Wilden Zwanziger. Der Architekt Laurent Bourgois und CS décoration arbeiteten, ausgehend von der klaren Linienführung der Architektur, Hand in Hand, um die Erwartungen ihres Kunden zu erfüllen. Es ist ihnen gelungen, in diesem luxuriösen und schnörkellosen Rahmen Werke zeitgenössischer Kunst auf elegante und humorvolle Weise mit außergewöhnlichen Möbelstücken des 20. Jahrhunderts zu kombinieren. Die Sachlichkeit der Lackoberflächen, die Auswahl des Marmors, die behutsame Bearbeitung der Holzarbeiten und die mit viel Fingerspitzengefühl durchgeführte Suche nach Teppichen und Stoffen stellen einen Hommage an die Sammlerstücke dar. „Stardust Memories", ein überlebensgroßes Gemälde von Christoph Ruckhäberle dominiert die Wand über einem einladenden elfenbeinfarbenen Sofa. Die klaren Linien des Barcelona-Couchtischs von Mies van der Rohe stehen schlichtend zwischen dem Rot der 1960er-Jahre-Sessel von Maxime Old und den indigoblauen Samthockern von Michel Boyer von 1968.

Situado en el elegante barrio parisino que se conoce como *le triangle d'or*, este apartamento podría ser la viva imagen de los felices años veinte y su decadencia. Sustentando su proyecto en líneas arquitectónicas puras, el arquitecto Laurent Bourgois y la agencia CS décoration consiguieron mediante su colaboración mutua cumplir las expectativas del cliente. En este rincón lujoso y sobrio lograron combinar con humor y elegancia obras de arte contemporáneas con mobiliario de excepción del siglo XX. La sobriedad de los lacados, la selección de los mármoles, el pulcro tratamiento de las obras de ebanistería y la búsqueda concienzuda de alfombras y tejidos rinden homenaje a todas estas piezas de colección. La inmensa creación "Stardust Memories" de Christoph Ruckhäberle parece volcarse sobre el cómodo sofá color crudo. La sobriedad de la mesa baja "Barcelona" de Mies van der Rohe hace contraste con el rojo de los sofás 1960 de Maxime Old y el azul índigo de los taburetes de Michel Boyer, creados en el año 1968.

Situato nell'elegantissimo quartiere parigino cosiddetto "Triangolo d'oro", questo *pied-à-terre* potrebbe incarnare lo spirito dei ruggenti anni '20 e della loro atmosfera decadente. Muovendo da un sistema di linee architettoniche pure, l'architetto Laurent Bourgois e CS décoration hanno trovato nella reciproca collaborazione una risposta alle esigenze del loro cliente. Tra le pareti di questo scrigno, nel contempo sobrio e lussuoso, sono riusciti con ironia ed eleganza ad abbinare opere d'arte contemporanee ad arredi e suppellettili d'eccezione del XX secolo. L'essenzialità delle lacche, la scelta dei marmi, l'accuratezza delle opere di falegnameria, la ricerca calibrata di tappeti e tessuti: tutto pare rendere omaggio a ciascun oggetto della collezione. L'iperbolico "Stardust Memories" di Christoph Ruckhäberle sembra rovesciarsi sulla confortevole morbidezza bianco crema del sofà. La severità del tavolino "Barcelona", di Mies van der Rohe, argina l'ondata scarlatta delle poltrone disegnate nel 1960 da Maxime Old e l'azzurro indaco dei tavolini di Michel Boyer (creati nel 1968).

In the guest bathroom, the use of white, black and yellow marble creates a linear graphic effect. This highlights the roundness of the white crystal sconces, designed by LB Studio and Caroline Sarkozy, which provide a dazzling glint. (The art deco Swedish Bench is by Folke Bensow.)

La salle de bains d'invités joue sur le graphisme linéaire des marbres de couleur blanche, noire et jaune, donnant à la rondeur des appliques murales en cristal blanc dessinées par LB Studio et Caroline Sarkozy un éclat singulier (banc suédois Art déco de Folke Bensow).

Das Gäste-Badezimmer spielt mit den grafischen Linien des weißen, schwarzen und gelben Marmors und hebt so die runde Form der weißen Kristall-Wandleuchten, die von LB Studio und Caroline Sarkozy entworfen wurden, besonders hervor (die schwedische Art déco-Bank stammt von Folke Bensow).

El cuarto de baño de invitados juega con el grafismo literario de los mármoles blancos, negros y amarillos y le otorga un brillo singular a la curvatura de los apliques de la pared de cristal blanco diseñados por LB Studio y Caroline Sarkozy (banco sueco art déco de Folke Bensow).

Il bagno degli ospiti gioca sul grafismo lineare dei marmi bianchi, neri e gialli, donando un inconsueto bagliore alla rotondità delle lampade a parete in cristallo bianco disegnate da LB Studio e Caroline Sarkozy (la panca art déco svedese è di Folke Bensow).

Country House in Paris

Auteuil

Makeup artist to the stars, Terry de Gunzburg worked closely with Yves Saint Laurent and later on created By Terry, her own brand of cosmetics. When she first acquired her art nouveau style home, it was entirely decorated disco style. With the decorative savoir faire of Jacques Grange, together they gave it a different soul: a country house in Paris, a home for her family and everything she finds beautiful. Since the kitchen is one of the most lived-in spaces, Jacques Grange, inspired by American kitchens from the 1940s, created a warm traditional family kitchen with oak cabinetry, an art deco inspired table with wicker chairs, and her collection of ceramics. The spaces were redistributed in a way where one room is an office, a dining room, a library, and a living room at once. Claude Lalanne sheep sculptures flank the garden and inhabit one of the dining areas. For Terry, what is most important for a home is its soul, the life it lives rather than it being a mere showcase of beautiful objects. It has to project the inner beauty of the family that lives within its walls.

Maquilleuse de stars, Terry de Gunzburg a étroitement collaboré avec Yves Saint Laurent pour ensuite créer By Terry, sa propre marque de produits de beauté. Lorsqu'elle a acheté sa maison de style Art nouveau, celle-ci était entièrement décorée dans le style disco. Grâce au savoir-faire du décorateur Jacques Grange, elle lui a donné une autre âme, celle d'une maison de campagne à Paris, d'un refuge pour sa famille et tout ce qu'elle trouve beau. La cuisine étant la pièce dans laquelle on séjourne le plus, Jacques Grange, imitant les cuisines américaines des années 1940, a créé une pièce familiale chaleureuse en combinant des meubles en chêne, une table d'inspiration Art déco, des chaises en osier et la collection de céramiques de Terry. L'espace a été redistribué de sorte qu'une même pièce sert à la fois de bureau, de salle à manger, de bibliothèque et de salon. Des moutons sculptés signés Claude Lalanne ornent le jardin et aussi un espace destiné à la restauration. Pour Terry, une maison n'est pas une simple vitrine pour de beaux objets, l'important c'est qu'elle ait une âme et qu'une vie l'anime : elle doit exprimer la beauté intérieure de la famille qui l'habite.

Die Star-Visagistin Terry de Gunzburg arbeitete eng mit Yves Saint Laurent zusammen und gründete später ihre eigene Kosmetiklinie By Terry. Als sie ihr neues Art nouveau-Haus erwarb, war es komplett im Disco-Stil eingerichtet. Zusammen mit Jacques Grange und seinem Savoir-faire in Bezug auf Einrichtungen verlieh sie dem Haus einen anderen Charakter und schuf ein Landhaus in Paris, ein Zuhause für ihre Familie und alles, was sie schön findet. Da die Küche einer der am häufigsten genutzten Räume ist, richtete Jacques Grange, inspiriert von amerikanischen Vorbildern der 1940er Jahre, eine warme, traditionelle Wohnküche mit Eichenschränken, einem vom Art déco inspirierten Tisch, Korbstühlen und de Gunzburgs Keramiksammlung ein. Die Raumaufteilung wurde komplett modifiziert, und es entstand ein Raum, der Arbeitsplatz, Esszimmer, Bibliothek und Wohnzimmer in einem ist. Schafskulpturen von Claude Lalanne stehen im Garten Spalier und tummeln sich neben einem der Essplätze. Das Wichtigste für Terry ist die Seele eines Hauses, dass Leben in ihm herrscht, statt nur ein Ausstellungsort für schöne Objekte zu sein. Es soll die innere Schönheit der Familie, die in diesen vier Wänden wohnt, nach außen sichtbar machen.

Terry de Gunzburg fue una maquilladora de estrellas. Trabajó estrechamente con Yves Saint Laurent y más tarde creó By Terry, su propia marca de cosméticos. Cuando adquirió su elegante casa modernista, estaba decorada por completo en estilo disco. Con la maestría decorativa de Jacques Grange, juntos dieron a la casa un alma diferente, crearon una casa de campo en París, un hogar para su familia y todo lo que ella considera hermoso. Ya que la cocina es uno de los espacios más frecuentados, Jacques Grange, inspirado por las cocinas americanas de los años 40, creó una cálida y tradicional cocina familiar con armario de roble, una mesa de inspiración art déco con sillas de mimbre y su colección de cerámica. Los espacios fueron redistribuidos de manera que una habitación sirve de oficina, comedor, librería y salón al mismo tiempo. Las esculturas con forma de oveja de Claude Lalanne flanquean el jardín y habitan una de las zonas pensadas como comedor. Para Terry, lo más importante en un hogar es su alma, su vida, en lugar de ser un mero escaparate de objetos bonitos. Debe proyectar la belleza interior de la familia que vive entre sus muros.

Truccatrice di dive e celebrità, Terry de Gunzburg è stata direttrice artistica del make-up Yves Saint Laurent e ha creato una propria linea di cosmetici chiamata By Terry. Quando acquistò la sua casa art nouveau, questa era paragonabile a un vero e proprio tempio del Disco style. In collaborazione con Jacques Grange, maestro di squisita raffinatezza, è riuscita a donarle una nuova fisionomia, a trasformarla in una residenza di campagna nel cuore di Parigi, a ricavarne uno spazio che accogliesse la sua famiglia e tutto il bello di cui ama circondarsi. Per la cucina, uno degli ambienti più vissuti di tutta la casa, Jacques Grange si è ispirato alle cucine americane degli anni '40 dando vita a un caldo ambiente tradizionale dove le armadiature in noce convivono con un tavolo d'ispirazione art déco incorniciato da sedie in midollino e con la collezione di ceramiche della padrona di casa. La ridistribuzione degli spazi ha permesso di ottenere un ambiente che è al tempo stesso studio, sala da pranzo, biblioteca e living. Attigue al giardino e in una delle zone pranzo campeggiano le pecore di Claude Lalanne. Per Terry ciò che conta veramente in una casa è la sua anima, la sua vita più autentica, non l'essere soltanto una vetrina di oggetti di buon gusto. E suo è il compito di progettare la bellezza interiore di coloro che hanno scelto di viverci.

This cozy dining area that opens to the winter garden displays table and chairs designed by Paul Frankl. This sitting room in fresh green hues features a Chinese carpet, lamps by Diego Giacometti and paintings by Richard Lindner.

La table et les chaises du douillet coin repas donnant sur le jardin d'hiver sont signées Paul Frankl. Le salon aux teintes vertes printanières est habillé d'un tapis chinois, de lampes de Diego Giacometti et de tableaux de Richard Lindner.

Der gemütliche Essplatz, der auf den Wintergarten hinausgeht, ist mit einem Tisch und Stühlen von Paul Frankl eingerichtet. Die in frischen Grüntönen gehaltene Sitzecke wurde mit einem chinesischen Teppich, Lampen von Diego Giacometti und Bildern von Richard Lindner dekoriert.

Esta agradable zona de comedor, la cual se abre hacia el jardín de invierno, exhibe mesa y sillas diseñadas por Paul Frankl. Este cuarto de estar en frescas tonalidades verdes vestido con alfombra china, lámparas de Diego Giacometti y pinturas de Richard Lindner.

La calda zona pranzo aperta sul giardino d'inverno è arredata con tavolo e sedie disegnati da Paul Frankl. Rivestita nelle fresche tonalità del verde, questa zona conversazione abbina un tappeto cinese a lampade di Diego Giacometti e quadri di Richard Lindner.

The bedroom walls are coated with Japanese style woven straw, floor parquetry and furniture all in golden hues. An armchair designed by Paul Iribe contrasts with a blue and black geometric rug by Zulhman.

Les murs de la chambre sont tendus de paille tissée dans le style japonais, et le parquet comme les meubles revêtent des teintes dorées. Un fauteuil dessiné par Paul Iribe s'oppose au tapis à motifs géométriques bleus et noirs signé Zulhman.

Im Schlafzimmer sind alle Wände mit gewebten Strohmatten im japanischen Stil bedeckt, Parkettboden und Möbel glänzen in Goldtönen. Ein Sessel von Paul Iribe hebt sich deutlich von einem blau-schwarzen Zulhman-Teppich mit geometrischem Muster ab.

Las paredes del dormitorio están cubiertas con paja tejida al estilo japonés, suelo con entarimado y mobiliario en tonalidades doradas. Sillón diseñado por Paul Iribe contrasta con una alfombra geométrica azul y negra de Zulhman.

Il canniccio intrecciato in stile giapponese che riveste le pareti della camera da letto crea una calda alchimia di tonalità dorate insieme al parquet del pavimento e agli elementi d'arredo. La poltrona di Paul Iribe contrasta il tappeto geometrico azzurro e nero di Zulhman.

Master's Hideaway

Saint-Germain-des-Prés

François Catroux debuted his career in 1967 when he was commissioned to decorate the haute couture house in Milan, Mila Schön. But for him, it really all started when he designed his own apartment, and ever since, he travels the world to decorate the residencies of his clients, celebrities and icons in the fashion world. He creates interiors that are comfortable and functional, yet refined with a timeless glamour—a sense of opulence and simplicity. His use of tones remain sober, while adding every here and there an object that brings out the light, whispering hints of colors, natural fibers and textures. In the study, bookshelf-lined walls accommodate a creamy velvet armchair and ottoman from the 1960s by Vladimir Kagan, and a one-of-a-kind 1920s André Arbus lacquered wood desk that stands under a Chinese lacquered painting of the Temple of Angkor by T'Choo from the 1930s. The entrance displays an imposing wooden framed sculpture of the tree of life and columns by Marcial Berro. A photo portrait of his wife Betty by Philippe de Lustrac covers one wall of the living room.

François Catroux débute sa carrière en 1967 avec l'aménagement de la maison de haute couture Mila Schön à Milan. Mais pour lui tout commence réellement avec la décoration de son propre appartement. Depuis, il parcourt le monde pour agencer les résidences de ses clients, célébrités et icônes du monde de la mode. Il crée des intérieurs confortables et fonctionnels, mais aussi raffinés et dotés d'une séduction intemporelle, mêlant richesse et simplicité. Sobre dans l'utilisation des couleurs, il ajoute ça et là un objet qui fait ressortir la lumière et affleurer des nuances de couleur, des fibres et des textures naturelles. Le bureau aux murs tapissés de rayons de bibliothèque abrite un fauteuil à dossier arrondi en corbeille crème en velours des années 1960 dessiné par Vladimir Kagan et un secrétaire des années 1920 en bois laqué unique en son genre d'André Arbus, surmonté d'une laque chinoise représentant le temple d'Angkor Vat, peinte par T'Choo dans les années 1930. Dans l'entrée, on peut admirer une imposante sculpture en bois représentant l'arbre de vie et des colonnes de Marcial Berro. Un portrait photographique de sa femme Betty par Philippe de Lustrac couvre l'un des murs du salon.

François Catrouxs Karriere begann 1967, als er den Auftrag bekam, das Haute-Couture-Haus Mila Schön in Mailand auszustatten. Für ihn selbst liegt der Anfang in der Einrichtung seiner eigenen Wohnung, und seither reist er um die Welt, um die Wohnsitze seiner Kunden, bekannte Namen und Ikonen der Modewelt, einzurichten. Er erzeugt behagliche und funktionale Innenausstattungen, die doch zugleich durch zeitlosen Glamour, eine gewisse Opulenz und Schlichtheit verfeinert sind. Er setzt Farben nur sehr nüchtern als unaufdringliche Akzente ein, fügt hier und da Objekte hinzu, die das Licht hervorheben, und nutzt erlesene Naturfasern und Texturen. Raumhohe Bücherregale ziehen sich über die Wände des Arbeitszimmers und bilden den Hintergrund für einen cremefarbenen Samtsessel mit Hocker von Vladimir Kagan aus den 1960er Jahren und einen einzigartigen 1920er Jahre Lack-Schreibtisch von André Arbus, der unter einem chinesischen Lackbild des Angkortempels von T'Choo aus den 1930er Jahren steht. In der Eingangshalle werden die Besucher von einer beeindruckenden Holzskulptur des Lebensbaumes und Säulen von Marcial Berro empfangen. Ein Porträtfoto Philippe de Lustracs von seiner Frau nimmt im Wohnzimmer eine ganze Wandseite ein.

François Catroux inició su carrera en 1967, cuando se le encargó la decoración de una casa de alta costura en Milán, Mila Schön. Sin embargo, para él todo comenzó en realidad cuando decoró su propio apartamento y, desde entonces, recorre el mundo para decorar las residencias de sus clientes, celebridades e iconos del mundo de la moda. Crea interiores cómodos, funcionales, aunque al mismo tiempo refinados, dotados de un encanto atemporal, un sentido de la opulencia y la simplicidad. Su uso de los tonos se mantiene sobrio, añadiendo aquí y allí un objeto que resalta la luz y susurra indicios de colores, fibras naturales y texturas. En el estudio, paredes pobladas de estantes para libros acomodan un sillón de terciopelo y un otomano color hueso años 60 de Vladimir Kagan, así como un exclusivo escritorio de madera lacada de André Arbus, años 20, que se encuentra bajo una pintura lacada china del Templo de Angkor firmada por T'Choo, años 30. La entrada muestra una imponente escultura de madera con forma del árbol de la vida y columnas de Marcial Berro. Una foto con el retrato de su mujer Betty de Philippe de Lustrac cubre una pared del salón.

La carriera di François Catroux ebbe inizio nel 1967, quando gli furono commissionati gli interni della sede milanese della maison d'alta moda Mila Schön. L'esperienza che tuttavia segnò il suo vero debutto fu la progettazione del proprio appartamento parigino; da allora, Catroux viaggia in tutto il mondo per arredare le abitazioni dei suoi clienti, che annoverano celebrità e icone del mondo della moda. I suoi interni sono confortevoli e funzionali, ma al tempo stesso raffinati e intrisi di un fascino senza tempo in cui il senso di opulenza si stempera nel rigore della semplicità. L'uso delle tonalità rimane sobrio nonostante la presenza occasionale di oggetti che accentuano la luminosità, in un lieve sussurrio di colori, fibre naturali e texture. Nello studio, le pareti rivestite di scaffalature incorniciano una poltrona in velluto color crema e un'ottomana anni '60 di Vladimir Kagan, con un prototipo di scrivania in legno laccato di André Arbus degli anni '20 cui fa da contrappunto, nella parete sovrastante, un pannello in lacca cinese realizzato da T'Choo negli anni '30 raffigurante il Tempio di Angkor. Nell'ingresso, inquadrata da una cornice, risalta la scultura in legno dell'albero della vita con colonne di Marcial Berro. Un ritratto di Betty, la moglie di Catroux, fotografata da Philippe de Lustrac, riveste quasi per intero una parete del living.

A magnificent glass and black lacquered wood desk that once belonged to André Arbus stands near the glass doors that open to the interior patio. One view of the living room shows lounge sofas designed by Catroux, with a round, black lacquered wood dining room table by Van Der Straeten and chairs by Philippe Starck. A unique African Dahomey mask hangs on one wall and a painting by James Brown on the other. Over the fireplace there is a star designed by Jansen in the 1940s–1950s.

Un magnifique secrétaire en verre et bois laqué noir ayant appartenu à André Arbus trône près des portes vitrées qui ouvrent sur le patio intérieur. Dans le salon, on peut admirer des chaises longues de Catroux, une table ronde laquée de noir dessinée par Van Der Straeten et des chaises créées par Philippe Starck. Un masque africain du Dahomey unique en son genre décore l'un des murs, alors qu'un tableau de James Brown orne le mur attenant. Au-dessus de la cheminée est suspendue une étoile, œuvre de Jansen des années 1940–1950.

Ein auffälliger Schreibtisch aus Glas und lackiertem Holz, der einst André Arbus gehörte, steht nahe der Fenstertüren, die in den Innenhof führen. Die beiden Chaiselongues im Wohnzimmer hat Catroux selbst entworfen, der runde Lack-Esstisch ist eine Schöpfung von Van Der Straeten und die Stühle sind von Philippe Starck. An der einen Wand hängt eine ungewöhnliche afrikanische Dahomey-Maske und an der anderen ein Gemälde von James Brown. Oberhalb des Kamins glänzt ein Stern, den Jansen etwa 1940–50 entwarf.

Un magnífico escritorio de cristal y madera lacada en negro que una vez perteneció a André Arbus' se halla junto a las puertas de cristal que se abren al patio interior. Una de las vistas del salón muestra sofás para tumbarse diseñados de Catroux, con una mesa de comedor de madera lacada en negro de Van Der Straeten y sillas de Philippe Starck. Una máscara africana dahomey única cuelga en una de las paredes y una pintura de James Brown en la otra. Sobre el hogar se encuentra una estrella diseñada por Jansen entre los años 40 y 50.

Una magnifica scrivania in cristallo e legno nero laccato, appartenuta ad André Arbus, precede le porte finestre che si aprono sul patio interno. Una prospettiva del living mostra divani lounge disegnati dallo stesso Catroux e, sullo sfondo, un tavolo da pranzo rotondo in legno laccato di Van Der Straeten con sedie di Philippe Starck. Su due pareti contigue spiccano un'originale maschera africana del Dahomey e un quadro di James Brown. Una scultura a stella di Jansen del decennio '40–'50 sovrasta il caminetto.

Hôtel de Gesvres

Bourse

When they first visited this four-room office suite, not far from the Paris Bourse, they suspected there was more to it than met the eye. The Hôtel de Gesvres is one of the two remaining mansions built by Louis XIV's architect Antoine Lepautre. Joseph Achkar and Michel Charrière, known for their passion and expertise of 17th-century architecture and interior design, were not only determined to bring the Hôtel de Gesvres back to life, they wanted to restore its soul. As partitions and false ceilings were removed, spacious rooms with original moldings and fretworks resurfaced. By the time they began peeling off layers of paint from walls and ceilings in the fourth room, the astonishing "cabinet of mirrors" was unearthed. Beautifully preserved golden-gilded panelings and pilasters, Versailles-style gallery of mirrors, ceiling frescos and mural motives created by the master artists of the period, stood there right before their eyes, as if time stood still.

Lorsqu'ils visitent ce complexe de bureaux à quatre salles non loin de la Bourse, ils soupçonnent l'endroit d'être bien plus riche qu'il ne le laisse paraître. L'hôtel de Gesvres est l'une des deux dernières demeures construites par Antoine Lepautre, l'architecte de Louis XIV. Connus pour leur passion et leur talent pour l'architecture du XVIIᵉ siècle et l'aménagement intérieur, Joseph Achkar et Michel Charrière sont alors résolus à faire revivre l'hôtel de Gesvres et à lui redonner son âme d'antan. Une fois retirés les séparations et les faux plafonds, des salles spacieuses ornées de moulures et de pièces chantournées originales refont surface. En dépouillant les murs et les plafonds de la quatrième pièce de multiples couches de peinture, ils exhument l'étonnant « cabinet aux miroirs ». Des panneaux et des colonnes dorés, des galeries de miroirs dans le style versaillais, des fresques de plafonds et des motifs muraux de grands maîtres de l'époque s'offrent à leurs yeux comme si le temps s'était arrêté.

Als sie dieses Büro, das sich unweit der Pariser Börse befindet, mit seinen vier Zimmern zum ersten Mal sahen, vermuteten sie bereits, dass mehr dahintersteckte. Das Hôtel de Gesvres ist eines von zwei erhaltenen Gebäuden des Architekten von Ludwig XIV., Antoine Lepautre. Joseph Achkar und Michel Charrière, bekannt für ihre Leidenschaft und Fachkenntnis der Architektur und Innenarchitektur des 17. Jahrhunderts, waren nicht nur entschlossen, das Hôtel de Gesvres wieder aufleben zu lassen, sondern auch seine Seele wiederherzustellen. Trennwände und Zwischendecken wurden entfernt. Dabei tauchten großzügige Räume mit Originalstuck und Holzornamenten wieder auf. Als sie begannen, die verschiedenen Farbschichten von den Wänden und Decken im vierten Raum abzutragen, trat ein erstaunliches „Spiegelkabinett" zutage. Sie erblickten wunderbar erhaltene, vergoldete Verkleidungen und Wandpfeiler, Spiegelgalerien im Stil von Versailles, Deckenfresken und Wandmotive, geschaffen von Spitzenkünstlern ihrer Zeit. Es war, als wäre die Zeit stehen geblieben.

La primera vez que visitaron esta suite de cuatro habitaciones separadas cerca de la Bolsa de París, sospecharon que había más en ella de lo que parecía en un principio. El Hôtel de Gesvres es una de las dos mansiones construidas por el arquitecto de Luis XIV, Antoine Lepautre, que han llegado a nuestros días. Joseph Achkar y Michel Charrière, conocidos por su pasión y experiencia en la arquitectura y el diseño de interiores del siglo XVII, no sólo estaban determinados a devolver el Hôtel de Gesvres a la vida, deseaban restaurar su alma. Una vez retirados los tabiques y los falsos techos, resurgieron las espaciosas habitaciones con molduras y calados originales. En el momento en el que empezaron a quitar capas de pintura de muros y techos en la cuarta habitación, el asombroso "gabinete de los espejos" salió a la luz. Paneles y pilares dorados hermosamente preservados, galería de espejos estilo Versalles, frescos en el techo y motivos murales creados por los expertos artistas del periodo, estaban allí justo frente a sus ojos, como si el tiempo se hubiera detenido.

La prima volta che videro questo studio di quattro stanze poco distante dalla Borsa di Parigi, Joseph Achkar e Michel Charrière sospettarono che dietro la sua facciata si celasse qualcosa in più di quello che appariva ai loro occhi. L'Hôtel de Gesvres è una delle due dimore ancora esistenti dell'architetto di Luigi XIV Antoine Lepautre. Achkar e Charrière, esperti conoscitori dell'architettura e dell'interior design del XVII secolo, hanno lavorato non soltanto per far risorgere l'Hôtel de Gesvres, ma anche per ricostituirne l'anima più autentica. La rimozione di tramezzi e controsoffitti ha restituito ampiezza alle sale decorate con stucchi e motivi a greca originali. Grazie al lavoro di eliminazione degli strati d'intonaco dalle pareti e dei soffitti dalla quarta stanza, è riemersa la stupefacente 'stanza degli specchi'. Davanti agli occhi di Joseph e Michel, in una sorta di momentanea sospensione temporale, si è materializzato un formidabile forziere di pannellature e colonne rivestiti in oro, un carosello di specchi degno di Versailles, uno scrigno di affreschi a soffitto e decorazioni murali frutto del genio dei più grandi maestri d'arte dell'epoca.

This view of the cabinet of mirrors shows richly elaborate 17ᵗʰ-century pilasters and wooden fretworks created by Claude Audran. The ceiling frescos and motifs were painted by a team of artists of the period: Jean Lepautre, Jean-Baptiste Belin de Fontenay, Alexandre-François Desportes, and Antoine Watteau.

Dans le cabinet aux miroirs, on peut admirer les colonnes et les pièces chantournées en bois du XVIIᵉ siècle signées Claude Audran. Les fresques du plafond et les motifs aux murs sont l'œuvre de divers artistes de l'époque, dont Jean Lepautre, Jean-Baptiste Belin de Fontenay, Alexandre-François Desportes et Antoine Watteau.

Dieser Blick auf das Spiegelkabinett zeigt aufwändig gearbeitete Wandpfeiler und Holzornamente aus dem 17. Jahrhundert, geschaffen von Claude Audran. Die Deckenfresken und Motive wurden von verschiedenen Künstlern aus dieser Zeit gemalt: Jean Lepautre, Jean-Baptiste Belin de Fontenay, Alexandre-François Desportes und Antoine Watteau.

Esta vista del gabinete de espejos muestra pilares del siglo XVII de rica elaboración y calados de madera creados por Claude Audran. Los frescos del techo y los motivos fueron pintados por un equipo de artistas de la época: Jean Lepautre, Jean-Baptiste Belin de Fontenay, Alexandre-François Desportes y Antoine Watteau.

Da questa prospettiva della stanza degli specchi emergono colonne del XVII secolo dai sontuosi ornamenti e motivi in legno intagliato creati da Claude Audran. Gli affreschi e gli ornamenti dei soffitti furono realizzati da un'équipe di artisti dell'epoca: Jean Lepautre, Jean-Baptiste Belin de Fontenay, Alexandre-François Desportes e Antoine Watteau.

Once the bedchamber to the Duc of Gesvres, a Louis XVI bed draped with silk fabric is surrounded by Louis XV chairs by Jean Avisse.

Dans l'ancienne chambre à coucher du duc de Gesvres, on peut admirer un lit Louis XVI tendu de soie, entouré de deux chaises Louis XV signées Jean Avisse.

Ein Bett aus der Zeit Ludwig XVI., einst Schlafgemach des Herzogs von Gesvres, drapiert mit Seide und umgeben von Stühlen aus der Zeit Ludwig XV. von Jean Avisse.

Una vez alcoba del Duque de Gesvres, una cama Louis XVI cubierta con tela de seda y rodeada por sillas Louis XV de Jean Avisse.

Nell'antica camera padronale del duca di Gesvres, il letto Luigi XVI drappeggiato con tessuto di seta è incorniciato da sedie Luigi XV di Jean Avisse.

Artist's Studio

Alésia

Sculptor, painter, designer, a creative jack-of-all-trades, Bernar Venet is also a collector: one who takes pleasure collecting the works of his French and American friends. Considered one of the pioneers of conceptual art and a major figure in New York's 1970s art scene, today, he's still on the move, working between his workshops in Hungary and Le Muy, France. For Bernar and his wife Diane, collector of jewelry by visual artists, their Parisian residence is more than just home; it is a platform where they establishes a dialogue between Bernar's own works and those of fellow artists to create an atmosphere of communion. For the past two decades, he has been designing furniture using his favorite prime material: raw iron. He bends it into chairs, stretches it out to sofas, and folds black tarnished cast iron into imposing dining room and coffee tables. The architectural structure itself is a conceptual expression where straight lines capsize into open spaces, doors are larger than life, and a spiraling staircase seeps through each level where artworks quiver on the walls and inhabit the grounds.

Sculpteur, peintre, designer, véritable touche-à-tout du monde de la création, Bernar Venet est aussi un collectionneur… un homme qui prend plaisir à rassembler les œuvres de ses amis français et américains. Considéré comme l'un des pionniers de l'art conceptuel et l'un des personnages clés du milieu artistique new-yorkais des années 1970, il demeure toujours aussi mobile et partage son temps entre ses ateliers de Hongrie et du Muy, dans le Var. Pour Bernar Venet et sa femme Diane, collectionneuse de bijoux d'artistes plasticiens, leur résidence parisienne est plus qu'une simple demeure. C'est la plateforme depuis laquelle ils établissent un dialogue entre les propres œuvres de Bernar et celles de leurs amis artistes pour créer une atmosphère de communion. Il a passé ces vingt dernières années à créer des meubles avec son matériau favori, l'acier brut : il le tord pour réaliser des chaises, l'étire pour concevoir des canapés et plie la fonte noircie pour en faire d'imposantes tables de salle à manger et de salon. La structure architecturale constitue en soi l'expression d'un concept : les lignes droites chavirent dans les espaces ouverts, les portes sont disproportionnées et l'escalier en colimaçon s'infiltre dans les différents niveaux, où les œuvres vibrantes sur les murs animent l'espace.

Bernar Venet ist Bildhauer, Maler, Designer, ein kreativer Alleskönner und Sammler … einer, der Freude daran hat, die Arbeiten seiner französischen und amerikanischen Freunde zu sammeln. Er gilt als einer der Pioniere der Konzeptkunst und zählt zu den wichtigsten Akteuren der New Yorker Kunstszene der 1970er Jahre. Auch heute noch ist er ständig unterwegs und arbeitet in seinen Ateliers in Ungarn und Le Muy, Frankreich. Ihre Pariser Wohnung ist aber für Bernar und seine Frau Diane Venet, die Schmuckstücke bildender Künstler sammelt, mehr als nur ein Zuhause. Sie ist das Podium, auf dem Bernars Werke mit denen seiner Künstlerfreunde einen Dialog eingehen und ein Gefühl von Zusammengehörigkeit erzeugen. In den vergangenen zwei Jahrzehnten entwarf er Möbel aus Roheisen, seinem Lieblingsmaterial, das er zu Stühlen biegt, zu Sofas auswalzt und in Form mattschwarzen Gusseisens zu mächtigen Ess- und Beistelltischen faltet. Die Architektur selbst wird zum Ausdruck des Konzeptuellen mit geraden Linien, die in weitläufige Räume übergehen, übergroßen Türen und einer spiralförmigen Treppe, die sich durch die einzelnen Geschosse windet, in denen Kunstwerke Boden und Wände beherrschen.

Escultor, pintor, diseñador, un multitalento creativo, Bernar Venet es también un coleccionista… alguien que disfruta coleccionando los trabajos de sus amigos franceses y estadounidenses. Considerado uno de los pioneros del arte conceptual y una de las figuras más destacadas de la escena artística neoyorkina de los años 70, todavía hoy se mantiene activo, trabajando a caballo entre sus talleres en Hungría y Le Muy, Francia. Para Bernar y su esposa Diane, coleccionista de joyería de artistas visuales, su residencia parisina es más que un hogar. Se trata de una plataforma donde establecen un diálogo entre los propios trabajos de Bernar y los de sus colegas artistas para crear una atmósfera de comunión. A lo largo de las dos últimas décadas se ha dedicado al diseño de mobiliario empleando su material principal preferido, el hierro en bruto, el cual dobla en forma de sillas, estira creando sofás, y pliega hierro fundido de negro deslustrado moldeando imponentes mesas de comedor y de café. La estructura arquitectónica es en sí misma una expresión conceptual en la que las líneas rectas se vuelcan en espacios abiertos, las puertas son más grandes que la vida y una escalera en espiral se filtra a través de cada planta, donde las ilustraciones se agitan en las paredes y habitan los jardines.

Scultore, pittore, designer, poliedrico factotum dall'estro creativo, Bernar Venet è anche collezionista… un genere di collezionista che ama raccogliere opere di artisti suoi amici, francesi e americani. Ritenuto uno dei pionieri dell'arte concettuale e annoverato tra i protagonisti di spicco del panorama artistico newyorkese degli anni '70, oggi, animato dalla passione di sempre, si divide tra il suo studio ungherese e quello di Le Muy, in Francia. Per Bernar e sua moglia Diane, collezionista di gioielli d'artista visiva, la loro residenza parigina è più che una semplice abitazione; è la piattaforma sulla quale entrambi riescono a imbastire un dialogo tra le opere di Bernar e quelle dei suoi compagni d'arte, al fine di creare un'atmosfera di comunione. Da vent'anni a questa parte Bernar disegna mobili utilizzando la materia prima che predilige, il ferro, che piega e allunga per ottenerne sedie e divani, incurvando la plumbea ghisa ossidata nella realizzazione di formidabili sale da pranzo e tavolini da caffè. La struttura architettonica stessa è un'espressione concettuale in cui le linee rette si rovesciano in spazi aperti, le porte assumono dimensioni esasperate e una scala spiraleggiante filtra attraverso i vari livelli, tra opere d'arte dall'effetto ottico vibrante che arricchiscono le pareti e riempiono gli spazi.

An upstairs second living room exhibits trilogy black and white painting by François Morellet and metal sculpture by Frank Stella.

Dans le deuxième salon à l'étage, on peut admirer la trilogie en noir et blanc de François Morellet et une sculpture en métal de Frank Stella.

In einem zweiten Wohnzimmer im Obergeschoss sind ein dreiteiliges schwarz-weißes Bild von François Morellet und eine Metallskulptur von Frank Stella ausgestellt.

Un segundo salón en la planta superior muestra trilogía pictórica en blanco y negro de François Morellet y escultura de metal de Frank Stella.

Nel secondo living al piano superiore dominano la scena una trilogia in bianco e nero di François Morellet e una scultura in metallo di Frank Stella.

Electric Ecclectic

Louvre

Early in his career, Pierre Passebon wrote about art and design. Some years later, he opened a space where he exhibited and sold artwork. It was with his lifetime partner, celebrated designer Jacques Grange, that he decided to create a common ground to display the objects of their shared artistic desires. A few steps from the gallery, this early 19th-century Directoire style flat is inlaid between two sumptuous courtyards. Mineral color tones were added to walls and ceilings to create height and luminosity. Initially, they wanted to give it a more baroque, exotic feeling but no matter what they tried, it didn't work. "It's like this place was holding on to its identity. It had a soul of its own." They played on the exchange of ideas, styles, a cross of medieval references, Amazonian headpieces, a Lion's mouth 16th-century Italian mantelpiece, contemporary furnishings from designers as Mattia Bonetti and Paul Poiret, and decorative objects by Lalanne, Laboureur and others.

Au début de sa carrière, Pierre Passebon écrit sur l'art et le design. Quelques années plus tard, il décide de créer avec son fidèle partenaire, le célèbre décorateur Jacques Grange, un lieu pour exposer le produit de leurs aspirations artistiques communes. À deux pas de cette galerie, l'appartement début XIXe de style Directoire est comme incrusté entre deux somptueuses cours intérieures. Des teintes minérales ont été ajoutées aux murs et aux plafonds pour conférer hauteur et luminosité. À l'origine, l'atmosphère devait être plus baroque et exotique, mais quels que soient leurs efforts, rien n'aboutissait. « C'est comme si ce lieu se cramponnait à sa propre identité, comme s'il avait une âme propre ». Ils ont alors joué sur l'association d'idées et de styles, combinant des références médiévales, des coiffes d'Amazonie, un manteau de cheminée italienne du XVIe en gueule de lion et des meubles contemporains de designers, tels que Mattia Bonetti, Paul Poiret, ainsi que des objets d'art de Lalanne, Laboureur et bien d'autres.

Zu Beginn seiner Karriere schrieb Pierre Passebon über Kunst und Design. Einige Jahre später eröffnete er eine Galerie, in der er Kunst ausstellte und verkaufte. Zusammen mit seinem Partner, dem gefeierten Designer Jacques Grange, traf er den Entschluss, die Objekte ihres geteilten künstlerischen Strebens gemeinsam auszustellen. Nur ein paar Schritte von der Galerie entfernt liegt diese Wohnung im Directoire-Stil aus dem frühen 19. Jahrhundert, eingeschmiegt zwischen zwei prächtigen Innenhöfen. Wände und Decken wurden in mineralischen Tönen gestrichen, um Höhe und Helligkeit zu schaffen. Ursprünglich wollten sie der Wohnung einen eher barocken, exotischen Stil verleihen, aber was auch immer sie unternahmen, es funktionierte nicht. „Dieser Ort hielt an seiner Identität fest. Er hat seinen eigenen Charakter." Also spielten sie mit wechselnden Ideen, Stilbrüchen, und Gegenüberstellungen mittelalterlicher Bezüge mit Amazonas-Kopfschmuck, einem italienischen Kamin des 16. Jahrhunderts in Form eines Löwenkopfes und zeitgenössischem Mobiliar von Designern wie Mattia Bonetti, Paul Poiret sowie Objekten von Lalanne, Laboureur und anderen.

En los comienzos de su carrera, Pierre Passebon escribió sobre arte y diseño. Algunos años más tarde, abrió un espacio en el que exhibía y vendía sus trabajos. Fue junto a su compañero de toda la vida, el celebrado diseñador Jacques Grange, con quien decidió crear un terreno conjunto para mostrar los objetos de sus deseos artísticos comunes. A unos pasos de la galería, este apartamento de estilo Directoire de principios del siglo XIX se ubica entre dos suntuosos patios. Se añadieron tonos minerales a paredes y techos para dar sensación de altura y luminosidad. Inicialmente, querían darle un sentimiento más barroco, exótico, pero daba igual lo que intentaran, no funcionaba. "Es como si este lugar se aferrara a su identidad. Tenía un alma propia". Jugaron con el intercambio de ideas, estilos, una mezcla de referencias medievales, coronas de plumas de la selva amazónica, una chimenea italiana con hogar en forma de cabeza de león del siglo XVI y muebles contemporáneos de diseñadores como Mattia Bonetti, Paul Poiret y objetos decorativos de Lalanne y Laboureur, entre otros.

All'inizio della sua carriera Pierre Passebon è stato autore di libri d'arte e di design. Alcuni anni più tardi ha aperto una galleria d'arte deputata all'esposizione e alla vendita delle sue opere realizzate in collaborazione col celebre designer Jacques Grange, partner di una vita assieme al quale ha deciso di creare un terreno d'intesa dove esporre gli oggetti frutto delle ambizioni artistiche condivise da entrambi. Situato a pochi passi dalla galleria, questo appartamento d'inizio del XIV secolo in stile Directoire è incastonato tra due sontuosi cortili. Le tonalità della pietra grezza, scelte per le pareti e i soffitti, creano verticalità e luminosità. Dopo un primo momento in cui i due artisti hanno cercato di conferire un'atmosfera più ridondante ed esotica agli ambienti, hanno dovuto desistere poiché nulla sembrava funzionare. "Era come se questa casa volesse restare fedele alla propria identità, come se avesse un carattere intrinseco". Hanno dunque mescolato idee e stili, giocato con elementi di derivazione medievale e copricapi amazzoni, abbinando a un caminetto a bocca di leone del XVI secolo italiano elementi d'arredo contemporanei di designer come Mattia Bonetti e Paul Poiret e oggetti decorativi di Lalanne, Laboureur e altri.

French style doors open the kitchen to the dining area. 19th-century tiles and porcelain from Portugal add a Mediterranean touch. A 1922 green lacquered cabinet by Paul Poiret showcases fine porcelain and two 19th-century bronze sculptures by Franz von Stuck.

La cuisine et le coin repas communiquent par des portes à la française. Un carrelage céramique XIXe siècle et des faïences du Portugal ajoutent une touche méditerranéenne. Une armoire laquée verte de 1922 de Paul Poiret contenant de la porcelaine fine est surmontée de deux bronzes XIXe de Franz von Stuck.

Türen im französischen Stil öffnen die Küche zum Esszimmer. Portugiesische Fliesen und Porzellan verleihen eine mediterrane Note. Ein grün lackierter Schrank von Paul Poiret aus dem Jahr 1922 stellt feines Porzellan und zwei Bronzestatuen von Franz von Stuck aus dem 19. Jahrhundert zur Schau.

Puertas de estilo francés abren la cocina hacia el comedor. Los azulejos del siglo XIX y la porcelana de Portugal añaden un toque mediterráneo. Una vitrina verde de 1922 de Paul Poiret expone porcelana fina y dos esculturas de bronce de Franz von Stuck del siglo XIX.

Porte francesi si aprono dalla cucina sulla zona pranzo. Le maioliche e la porcellana portoghese del XIX secolo aggiungono un tocco mediterraneo. Una vetrinetta laccata verde del 1922 di Paul Poiret esibisce raffinate porcellane e due sculture in bronzo del XIX di Franz von Stuck.

This living room perspective shows a pair of marble top 18th-century armoires signed Moreau. The white obelisk shaped sculptures are Omaggio a Melotti by Gio Ponti.

Cette vue du salon permet d'admirer deux armoires XVIIIe à dessus en marbre de Moreau. Les sculptures en forme d'obélisque sont un exemplaire de « Omaggio a Melotti » de Gio Ponti.

Im Wohnzimmer erblickt man zwei Schränke mit Marmorplatten von Moreau aus dem 18. Jahrhundert. Die weißen, wie Obeliske geformten Skulpturen heißen „Omaggio a Melotti" von Gio Ponti.

Esta perspectiva del salón muestra una pareja de armarios con cubierta de mármol del siglo XVIII firmados por Moreau. Las esculturas con forma de obelisco blanco son "Omaggio a Melotti" por Gio Ponti.

Da questa prospettiva del soggiorno s'intravede una coppia di armadi settecenteschi con la parte superiore di marmo firmati Moreau. L'insieme delle sculture bianche a obelisco dal titolo "Omaggio a Melotti" è di Gio Ponti.

Cosmopolitan Soul

Saint-Germain-des-Prés

The *hôtel particulier* is tucked away in a parcel of gardens, past an inner courtyard and behind a monumental iron gate. Gisèle Ghanem of Laurent Bourgois Architecte teamed up with London-based designers Collett-Zarzycki to create what Laurent Bourgois describes as *haute couture*. At first sight, one may have the impression of looking at a juxtaposition of colors and styles, but a second careful glance allows you to see the creative thought behind it and the symmetry of its composition. Original architectural spaces and structures on the lower levels remain, while the upper floors were metamorphosed giving the impression that each flight of stairs leads into a different house. The designers created most of the furniture in rich fabrics and textures, keeping coherence within the eclectic by adding touches of decorative objects found in flea markets and antique shops. Artwork from the owner's personal collection gives this *trés* Parisian *pied-à-terre* a cosmopolitan soul.

L'hôtel particulier est lové dans un ensemble de jardins, derrière une cour intérieure fermée par un monumental portail en fer forgé. Ce projet a été suivi par Gisèle Ghanem pour Laurent Bourgois Architecte. Le cabinet d'architecture a travaillé en partenariat avec Collett-Zarzycki, décorateur londonien, pour créer ce que Laurent Bourgois décrit comme un projet « haute couture ». L'ensemble donne tout d'abord l'impression d'une juxtaposition de couleurs et de styles désorganisée, mais l'on peut découvrir au second regard plus attentif l'idée créatrice qui le porte et la symétrie de la composition. Si les volumes et les structures architecturales des niveaux inférieurs ont été conservés, les étages supérieurs ont été transformés, et l'on a ainsi l'impression que chaque volée d'escalier conduit à une maison différente. Les décorateurs ont créé l'essentiel des meubles à partir d'étoffes et de textures précieuses, tout en restant cohérent dans l'éclectisme grâce à quelques objets décoratifs dénichés dans des marchés aux puces ou chez des antiquaires. Des œuvres d'art de la collection personnelle du propriétaire donnent à ce « pied-à-terre » très parisien une âme cosmopolite.

Diese Stadtvilla liegt inmitten von Gärten, verborgen am Ende eines Innenhofes und hinter einem monumentalen schmiedeeisernen Tor. Gisèle Ghanem von Laurent Bourgois Architecte arbeitete mit den Londoner Designern von Collett-Zarzycki zusammen, um etwas zu schaffen, was Laurent Bourgois als Haute Couture beschreibt. Zuerst hat man den Eindruck eines Durcheinanders verschiedener Farben und Stile, ein zweiter aufmerksamer Blick lässt dann jedoch den kreativen Schöpfungsgedanken und die Symmetrie der Komposition erkennen. In den unteren Geschossen blieben Raumvolumina und Struktur der Architektur erhalten, die Obergeschosse jedoch wurden so umgestaltet, dass man den Eindruck bekommt, jeder Treppenabsatz führe in ein anderes Haus. Die Designer entwarfen die meisten Möbelstücke mit edlen Stoffen und Texturen und verbanden den eklektischen Stil durch vereinzelt hinzugefügte, auf dem Flohmarkt und bei Antiquitätenhändlern entdeckte Deko-Objekte. Kunstwerke aus der persönlichen Sammlung des Eigentümers verleihen diesem *pied-à-terre* einen kosmopoliten Charakter.

El *hôtel particulier* se encuentra bien resguardado en una parcela de jardines, pasando un patio interno y tras una puerta monumental de hierro fundido. Gisèle Ghanem se ha encargado de este proyecto para Laurent Bourgois Architecte. La agencia de arquitectura trabajó en colaboración con los decoradores londinenses Collett-Zarzycki para crear lo que Laurent Bourgois describe como un proyecto *haute couture*. El conjunto da en un primer momento la sensación de estar observando una yuxtaposición de colores y estilos desorganizada, pero una segunda mirada cuidadosa permite apreciar el pensamiento creativo subyacente y la simetría de su composición. Los volúmenes y las estructuras originales de los niveles inferiores fueron conservadas, mientras los pisos superiores fueron transformados de tal forma que da la impresión de que cada tramo de escaleras conduce a una casa diferente. Los decoradores crearon la mayor parte del mobiliario en ricos tejidos y texturas, manteniendo la coherencia dentro de lo ecléctico al añadir toques con objetos decorativos que proceden de rastros y tiendas de antigüedades. Las ilustraciones de la colección personal del propietario dan a este muy parisino *pied-à-terre* un alma cosmopolita.

L'hôtel particulier s'intravede tra le fronde di un giardino al di là di un cortile interno, dietro a un'imponente cancellata in ferro battuto. Questo progetto è stato supervisionato da Gisèle Ghanam per Laurent Bourgois Architecte. Lo studio di architettura ha collaborato in tandem con il designer londinese Collett-Zarzycki per creare quello che Laurent Bourgois definisce un progetto di *haute couture*. L'insieme a prima vista può apparire un semplice accostamento disorganizzato di colori e stili ma, a uno sguardo più attento, rivela la genialità che lo ha prodotto e la simmetria della sua composizione. Ai piani inferiori sono stati conservati i volumi e le strutture originali, mentre quelli superiori hanno subito un mutamento radicale, tale da dare l'impressione che ogni scalinata conduca a una casa diversa. I decoratori hanno realizzato gran parte del mobilio con tessuti e texture pregiati, mantenendosi fedeli allo stile eclettico con l'introduzione di oggetti decorativi scovati nei mercatini e nelle botteghe d'antiquariato. Le opere della collezione personale del proprietario conferiscono un'anima cosmopolita a questo *pied-à-terre* così squisitamente parigino.

A winding staircase leads to a 19th-century mosaic marble floor restored by Delphine Messmer. Madame's office fashions a mahogany desk and armoire designed by Collett-Zarzycki.

Un escalier en colimaçon conduit à la mosaïque de marbre du parterre XIXe rénové par Delphine Messmer. Le bureau de madame s'enorgueillit d'un secrétaire en acajou et d'une armoire dessinée par Collett-Zarzycki.

Die geschwungene Treppe führt zu dem von Delphine Messmer restaurierten marmornen Mosaikboden aus dem 19. Jahrhundert. Das Arbeitszimmer von Madame zieren ein Schreibtisch und ein Schrank aus Mahagoniholz von Collett-Zarzycki.

Una sinuosa escalera conduce al suelo de mármol en mosaico del siglo XIX, restaurado por Delphine Messmer. La oficina de Madame contiene un escritorio y un armario de caoba diseñados por Collett-Zarzycki.

Una scala spiraleggiante conduce a un pavimento in mosaico del XIX secolo restaurato da Delphine Messmer. Nell'ufficio di Madame spiccano una scrivania in mogano e un armadio disegnati da Collett-Zarzycki.

The master bedroom displays the owner's collection of contemporary art. The attic is transformed into an open-loft style studio/bedroom for their teenage daughter.

La chambre de maître permet d'admirer la collection d'art contemporain du propriétaire. Le grenier est transformé en une chambre style loft pour leur fille encore adolescente.

Teile der Kunstsammlung des Eigentümers werden im Elternschlafzimmer ausgestellt. Das Dachgeschoss verwandelte sich in ein loftartiges offenes Studio für die Tochter im Teenageralter.

El dormitorio principal muestra la colección de arte contemporáneo del propietario. El ático se ha transformado en un dormitorio estilo estudio loft abierto para su hija adolescente.

La camera padronale ospita la collezione d'arte contemporanea del proprietario. L'attico è stato trasformato per la figlia adolescente in una camera da letto stile open space che pare quasi un monolocale.

Old Printing House

Saint-Germain-des-Prés

Approaching the front gate of the classic Haussmannian building, we make the unbelievable discovery of an English cottage across the courtyard. The unusual monastic style house was a printing press during the French Revolution. Caroline Sarkozy and Guillaume Cochin brought their client's dream to life. They met the challenge of renovating a family home that is both refined and tastefully decorated. Caroline succeeds in displaying their exceptional art collection at its best. Outside, the expanse of greenery has been transformed into an English garden with French touches. The small lounge, the only room where the original beams have been retained, was the starting point for the restoration. Contemporary artists, Jean-Michel Alberola and Nicolas and Sébastien Reese's studio, were hired to create bespoke murals for the lounge, which are interchangeable due to their integrated reversible panels. The idea was to blend styles and contrast time periods. The portrait of Albert Einstein by Bernard Pras and the harp chair by Jorgen Hovelskov brings a fresh, modern element to the lounge.

À peine a-t-on franchi la porte d'entrée d'un bâtiment haussmannien classique et traversé son arrière-cour que l'on découvre un improbable mais authentique cottage anglais. Cette habitation atypique de style monacal était une imprimerie durant la Révolution française. Caroline Sarkozy et Guillaume Cochin ont donné corps au rêve de leur cliente. Ils ont réussi le pari de recréer une maison familiale à la fois raffinée et décorée avec goût où Caroline a su mettre en valeur leur importante collection d'oeuvres d'art. Pour l'extérieur, l'espace de verdure a été transformé en jardin anglais aux accents français. Le petit salon, seule pièce ayant conservée ses boiseries d'origine, a été le point de départ de cette réhabilitation. Les artistes contemporains, Jean-Michel Alberola et le Studio de Nicolas et Sébastien Reese, se sont employés à y réaliser sur mesure des décors muraux se substituant l'un à l'autre grâce à des panneaux chantournés réversibles. L'idée était de créer un espace alliant des styles et des époques contrastés. Une note de fraîcheur et de modernité est apportée au salon avec le portrait d'Albert Einstein par Bernard Pras et une chaise harpe de Jorgen Hovelskov.

Nachdem man durch die Eingangstür eines typischen Haussmann-Gebäudes getreten ist und einen Innenhof durchquert hat, entdeckt man überraschenderweise ein echtes englisches Cottage. In dieser untypischen Behausung, die an ein Kloster erinnert, wurde während der französischen Revolution eine Druckerei betrieben. Caroline Sarkozy und Guillaume Cochin erfüllten ihren Kunden einen Traum und richteten ein Zuhause für eine Familie ein, das raffiniert und gleichzeitig sehr geschmackvoll ist, und in dem Caroline die bedeutende Kunstsammlung zur Geltung brachte. Der Garten wurde in einen englischen Garten mit französischer Note umgewandelt. Der kleine Salon, der einzige Raum, in dem der originale Holzboden erhalten geblieben war, wurde zum Ausgangspunkt für die Renovierung. Die zeitgenössischen Künstler Jean-Michel Alberola und das Studio von Nicolas und Sébastien Reese haben speziell für diesen Raum einen Wandschmuck aus Holzpaneelen entworfen, der es ermöglicht, mal das Werk des einen, mal das des anderen zu zeigen. Die Idee hinter dieser Einrichtung ist, gegensätzliche Stile und Epochen miteinander zu vereinen. Der Wohnraum erhält durch ein Porträtbild Albert Einsteins von Bernard Pras und einen Harfensessel von Jorgen Hovelskov eine frische und moderne Note.

Tan pronto como se abre la puerta de entrada de un edificio haussmaniano clásico y se cruza su patio trasero, se descubre una inusual pero auténtica casita inglesa. Esta vivienda atípica de estilo monacal fue una imprenta durante la Revolución Francesa. Caroline Sarkozy y Guillaume Cochin han dado vida al sueño de su cliente. Entre los dos han superado el reto de recrear una casa familiar refinada y, al mismo tiempo, decorada con gusto en la que Caroline ha sabido poner de relieve su importante colección de obras de arte. En el exterior, el espacio de verdor se ha transformado en un jardín inglés con notas francesas. El pequeño salón, la única habitación que ha conservado sus paneles de madera originales, ha sido el punto de partida de esta reforma. Los artistas contemporáneos, Jean-Michel Alberola y el Estudio de Nicolas y Sébastien Reese, trabajaron en la realización de decorados murales a medida que se sustituyen los unos a los otros por medio de paneles contorneados reversibles. La idea consistía en crear un espacio que combinase estilos y épocas en contraste. Un retrato de Albert Einstein de Bernard Pras y una silla arpa de Jorgen Hovelskov aportan un toque de frescura y modernidad al salón.

Varcata la soglia d'ingresso di un tipico edificio Haussmann, al di là del cortile, si scopre un improbabile ma autentico cottage inglese. Nella Francia della Rivoluzione, le mura di questa dimora dallo stile insolitamente severo ospitavano una stamperia. Caroline Sarkozy e Guillaume Cochin hanno saputo dar forma al desiderio del loro cliente, ricreando una casa pensata per una famiglia che fosse al tempo stesso raffinata e sapientemente guarnita, in cui Caroline ha saputo valorizzare l'importante collezione d'arte dei padroni di casa. All'esterno, le macchie di vegetazione sono state ridisegnate in un giardino all'inglese che lascia spazio ad accenti francesi. Il salotto, l'unica stanza ad aver conservato la boiserie originale, è stato il punto di partenza dell'opera di restauro. Un team di artisti contemporanei, Jean-Michel Alberola e lo Studio de Nicolas et Sébastien Reese, ha realizzato su misura elementi decorativi murali intercambiabili grazie a una serie di pannelli traforati reversibili. L'obiettivo era creare uno spazio che potesse rivestirsi di stili o riecheggiare epoche contrastanti. Una nota di freschezza e modernità ha riempito il living con l'inserimento di un ritratto di Albert Einstein di Bernard Pras dietro a una sedia ad arpa di Jorgen Hovelskov.

In the lounge, the paintings by Andy Warhol and Olivier Debré frame the entrance to the small lounge. Art deco inspired armchairs proudly sit between a Mies van der Rohe coffee table and a headless leather cow sculpture by Julia Lohmann.

Dans le salon, le tableau d'Andy Warhol et celui d'Olivier Debré encadrent le passage vers le petit salon. Des fauteuils Art déco trônent entre une table basse de Mies van der Rohe et une vache en cuir sans tête de Julia Lohmann.

Dieser Blick ins Wohnzimmer zeigt ein Andy-Warhol-Gemälde auf der rechten Seite des Durchgangs zum kleinen Salon und ein Bild Olivier Debrés auf der linken. Art déco-Sessel wurden zwischen einem Couchtisch von Mies van der Rohe und einer kopflosen ledernen Kuhskulptur von Julia Lohmann platziert.

En el salón, los cuadros de Andy Warhol y Olivier Debré flanquean el paso hacia el pequeño salón. Sillones art déco destacan entre una mesa baja de Mies van der Rohe y una vaca de cuero sin cabeza de Julia Lohmann.

Nel living, i quadri di Andy Warhol e Olivier Debré inquadrano il passaggio verso il salotto. Due poltroncine art déco fanno da cornice a un coffee-table di Mies van der Rohe accanto alla scultura acefala di una mucca, opera di Julia Lohmann.

The reversible panels adorning the dining room provide a different atmosphere at every meal. One side was painted by Jean-Michel Alberola, the other by the studio of Nicolas and Sébastien Reese, who revisited a classic 18th-century image of a monkey.

Les panneaux chantournés réversibles décorant la salle à manger donnent à chaque dîner une ambiance différente. Une face a été peinte par Jean-Michel Alberola et l'autre par le Studio de Nicolas et Sébastien Reese, qui a revisité le motif classique du singe du XVIIIᵉ siècle.

Die Holzpaneele im Esszimmer können gewendet werden und verändern die Wirkung des Raumes anlässlich jedes Abendessens. Eine Seite wurde von Jean-Michel Alberola bemalt, die andere vom Studio Nicolas und Sébastien Reeses, die ein klassisches Affenmotiv des 18. Jahrhunderts wieder aufgriffen.

Los paneles contorneados reversibles que decoran el comedor crean un ambiente distinto para cada cena. Uno de los retratos es obra de Jean-Michel Alberola y el otro lo firma el Estudio de Nicolas y Sébastien Reese, que ha retomado el motivo clásico del mono del siglo XVIII.

I pannelli traforati reversibili della sala da pranzo creano un ambiente diverso a seconda del convivio. Jean-Michel Alberola ne ha dipinta una superficie, l'altra è opera dello Studio de Nicolas et Sébastien Reese, che ha rivisitato il motivo classico della scimmia in voga nel XVIII secolo.

In the entrance hall, the monkey head sculpted by Jean-Marie Fiori adorns the lacquered wood table designed by Jules Leleu and Jean Prouvé in the 1950s.

Dans l'entrée, la tête de singe sculptée par Jean-Marie Fiori orne la table au pied en bois laqué dessiné par Jules Leleu et Jean Prouvé dans les années 1950.

Im Eingangsbereich ziert eine Affenkopfskulptur von Jean-Marie Fiori den Tisch mit Lackbeinen, der in den 1950er Jahren von Jules Leleu und Jean Prouvé entworfen wurde.

En la entrada, la cabeza de mono esculpida por Jean-Marie Fiori decora la mesa con pie de madera lacada diseñada por Jules Leleu y Jean Prouvé en los años 50.

Nell'ingresso, la testa di scimmia scolpita di Jean-Marie Fiori troneggia sul tavolo in legno laccato disegnato da Jules Leleu e Jean Prouvé negli anni '50.

Garden of Eden

Place des Victoires

For Hubert Le Gall it all started in his early years as a painter, when he itched to find a medium that would set his creative forces free and bring his wildest dreams to life. Today as a designer, he creates objects of wonder: his Flora and Fauna creations branch out to pieces based on a poetic bestiary where a heron lamp stands on a bull cabinet, and his daisy tables and flower commodes have become emblematic to the new meaning he has given to furniture and decorative arts. When he was commissioned to decorate this Parisian flat, he used the palettes of natural beiges and grays as a backdrop for his surrealist forest, rich in colors, textures, light reflections, and gold. In the living room he sets his velvet Whale armchair in front of a gold-leaf and mirror commode, crested with a ceramic sculpture lamp by Guidette Carbonell, circa 1950, a Murano vase, and a Jean René Gauguin animal ceramic from the 1920s.

Pour Hubert Le Gall, tout a commencé dans ses jeunes années, alors qu'il était peintre et qu'il cherchait avidement un support pour donner libre cours à ses forces créatives et concrétiser ses rêves les plus fous. Aujourd'hui, ce designer crée des objets qui suscitent l'étonnement. Ses créations sur la flore et la faune se traduisent par des œuvres très diverses inspirées d'un bestiaire poétique : une lampe héron trônant sur un cabinet taureau, des tables marguerites et des commodes fleuries illustrent la nouvelle signification qu'il a insufflé aux meubles et aux arts décoratifs. Lorsqu'on lui a demandé de décorer cet appartement parisien, il a utilisé des palettes de beiges et de gris naturels comme toile de fond pour sa forêt surréaliste aux nombreuses couleurs, textures, réflexions de lumière et dorures. Dans le salon, il a placé son fauteuil baleine en velours face à une commode en bois plaqué de feuilles d'or jaune et de miroirs, laquelle est couronnée d'une lampe sculptée en céramique créée par Guidette Carbonell vers 1950, d'un vase Murano et d'un animal en céramique de Jean René Gauguin des années 1920.

Als Hubert Le Gall in jungen Jahren Maler war, wollte er unbedingt ein Medium finden, in dem er seine kreativen Kräfte besser freisetzen und seine kühnsten Träume verwirklichen konnte. So wurde er schließlich Designer und bringt heute wundersame Objekte hervor. Seine Flora- und Fauna-Schöpfungen formen sich zu Gegenständen, die einem poetischen Bestiarium entstammen: eine Reiher-Lampe steht auf einem Stier-Tisch, und seine Gänseblümchen-Tische und Blüten-Kommoden sind Sinnbild der neuen Bedeutung geworden, die er Mobiliar und Kunsthandwerk gegeben hat. Als er den Auftrag bekam, diese Pariser Wohnung einzurichten, setzte er natürliche Beige- und Grautöne als Hintergrund ein für einen farbenfrohen, surrealen Wald, mit prachtvollen Texturen, Lichtreflexen und viel Gold. Im Wohnzimmer platzierte er seinen Wal-Sessel gegenüber einer Kommode aus Blattgold und Spiegeln, die von einer Lampenskulptur aus Keramik von Guidette Carbonell, um 1950, einer Murano-Vase und einem Keramiktier von Jean René Gauguin aus den 1920er Jahren geziert wird.

Para Hubert Le Gall todo empezó en sus primeros años como pintor, cuando deseaba con ansia encontrar un medio capaz de liberar su fuerza creativa y hacer realidad sus sueños más salvajes. Hoy en día, da forma a objetos de admiración como diseñador, sus creaciones de flora y fauna se diversifican en piezas basadas en un bestiario poético, donde una lámpara con forma de garza está colocada sobre un gabinete de toro y sus mesas de margarita y cómodas en forma de flor se convierten en emblemas del nuevo significado que ha conferido al arte del mobiliario y la decoración. Cuando se le encomendó decorar este apartamento parisino, recurrió a las paletas de beiges y grises naturales como telón de fondo para su bosque surrealista, rico en colores, texturas, reflejos de luz y oro. En el salón coloca su sillón ballena de terciopelo frente a la cómoda de hojas doradas y espejo, coronada por una lámpara-escultura de cerámica de Guidette Carbonell, aproximadamente de 1950, un florero Murano y una cerámica con forma de animal Jean René Gauguin de los años 20.

Per Hubert Le Gall tutto ebbe inizio nei primi anni della sua carriera di pittore, quando avvertì la necessità impellente di trovare un mezzo capace di sprigionare le sue forze creative e dar vita ai suoi sogni più audaci. Oggi, nel suo ruolo di designer plasma oggetti prodigiosi, le sue creazioni si traducono in pezzi ispirati a un poetico bestiario in cui una lampada dalle fattezze di un airone poggia su uno armadietto a corna d'ariete, mentre i tavoli margherita e i cassettoni fiore sono diventati l'emblema del significato tutto inedito di cui La Gall ha voluto rivestire l'arredamento e le arti decorative. Per realizzare gli interni di questo appartamento parigino ha utilizzato la tavolozza dei beige e dei grigi naturali come sfondo della sua surreale foresta, ricca di colori, texture, riflessi di luce e oro. Nel living ha scelto di collocare la poltrona in velluto Whale di sua creazione di fronte a un cassettone rivestito a specchio e lamina d'oro, su cui troneggiano una lampada-scultura di ceramica di Guidette Carbonell del 1950 circa, un vaso di Murano e un animale di ceramica disegnato da Jean René Gauguin negli anni '20.

In the bedroom, the bed is dressed in leather and faux fur flanked by metal night tables by India Mahdavi. The mirror wall lamps are a Hubert Le Gall design. Under the wood and inox staircase stands an iron and leather desk (c. 1980) by André Dubreuil and Tom Dixon, adorned with ceramics by Guidette Carbonell, a bronze candelabra, and a skull by Hubert Le Gall.

Dans la chambre, le lit tendu de cuir et de fourrure d'imitation est flanqué de tables de nuit en métal d'India Mahdavi. Les appliques murales miroir sont d'Hubert Le Gall. Sous l'escalier bois-inox trône un bureau mêlant fer et cuir d'André Dubreuil et Tom Dixon de 1980 que viennent orner des céramiques de Guidette Carbonell, un chandelier en bronze et un crâne d'Hubert Le Gall.

Das Bett im Schlafzimmer hüllt sich in Leder und künstlichen Pelz und wird von metallenen Nachttischen von India Mahdavi flankiert. Die Spiegel-Wandlampen sind ein Entwurf Hubert Le Galls. Unter der Treppe aus Holz und Edelstahl steht ein Tisch aus Eisen und Leder von André Dubreuil und Tom Dixon. Er ist mit Keramiken von Guidette Carbonell, einem Bronzeleuchter und einem Schädel von Hubert Le Gall dekoriert.

En el dormitorio, la cama está vestida con cuero e imitación de piel y flanqueada por mesitas de noche de metal de India Mahdavi. Las lámparas de pared de espejo son un diseño de Hubert Le Gall. Bajo la escalera de madera y acero inoxidable se encuentra un escritorio de hierro y cuero de André Dubreuil y Tom Dixon, 1980, ornamentado con cerámicas de Guidette Carbonell, lámpara de araña de bronce y cráneo de Hubert Le Gall.

Nella camera padronale, il letto rivestito in pelle e finta pelliccia è cinto da comodini in metallo di India Mahdavi. Le lampade a muro con supporto a specchio sono una creazione di Hubert Le Gall. Sovrastata dalla scala in legno e inox, la scrivania in ferro e cuoio di André Dubreuil e Tom Dixon (1980) regge ceramiche di Guidette Carbonell, due candelieri in bronzo e un teschio di Hubert Le Gall.

Secret Garden

Montparnasse

"In our search for somewhere we would be happy to live, we were hoping to track down an exceptionally bright apartment in Paris. However, upon visiting this 19ᵗʰ-century studio, it was love at first sight!" With the help of architect, Jacques Danan, Caroline Sarkozy entirely renovated the studio. From the renovation of the building's façade, redesign of the flooring and living areas to the restored deteriorated elements, the original style of the period was preserved. She has provided the residence with a subtle and timeless charm whilst remaining faithful to its history and artistic spirit. Caroline combines furniture that her family has owned for generations with original pieces from her favorite artists and craftsmen. She has taken great care in creating a home that is a reflection of herself—a home with a soul. We wander with delight among the souvenirs from her travels, her favorite possessions, and works by contemporary artists and designers. The house opens out to a landscaped garden of boxed hedges, created by the talented May de Lasteyrie, drawing inspiration from Caroline's childhood in Georgetown.

« En cherchant un endroit dans lequel nous pourrions vivre, nous espérions dénicher un appartement très lumineux dans Paris. Mais lorsque nous avons visité cet atelier d'artiste du XIXᵉ siècle, cela a été le coup de foudre ! » Avec l'aide de l'architecte Jacques Danan, Caroline Sarkozy a entièrement réhabilité l'atelier. La rehausse de la façade extérieure, le remaniement des planchers et des espaces de vie jusqu'à la restauration des éléments détériorés lui ont redonné son cachet d'époque. Elle a su donner à ce lieu un charme familial et intemporel en restant fidèle à son histoire et à son énergie artistique. Caroline associe des meubles appartenant à sa famille depuis plusieurs générations aux créations originales de ses artistes et artisans favoris. Elle s'est appliquée à se créer un « chez soi » qui lui ressemble, qui possède une âme. On se promène avec délectation entre ses souvenirs de voyage, ses objets préférés et les œuvres d'artistes et de designers contemporains. La maison s'ouvre sur un jardin de massifs de buis composé par la talentueuse paysagiste May de Lasteyrie s'inspirant de l'enfance de Caroline à Georgetown.

„Als wir eine Wohnung suchten, die unser neues Zuhause sein sollte, hofften wir, ein vom Licht überflutetes Apartment zu finden. Aber als wir dieses Künstleratelier aus dem 19. Jahrhundert entdeckten, war es Liebe auf den ersten Blick!" In Zusammenarbeit mit dem Architekten Jacques Danan hat Caroline Sarkozy das Atelier komplett renoviert. Durch das Aufarbeiten der Fassade, die Renovierung der Holzböden und die Modifikation der Raumaufteilung bis hin zur Nachbildung zerstörter Elemente, konnte der Geist der Epoche wiederhergestellt werden. Sie hat es geschafft, diesem Haus einen familiären und zeitlosen Charme zu verleihen und gleichzeitig der Geschichte des Ortes und seiner künstlerischen Energie treu zu bleiben. Caroline Sarkozy kombiniert Möbelstücke, die seit mehreren Generationen im Familienbesitz sind, mit originellen Objekten ihrer Lieblingskünstler und -kunsthandwerker. Es war ihr Ziel, für sich selbst ein Zuhause zu schaffen, das ihr ähnelt und das eine Seele hat. Es ist ein Vergnügen, zwischen ihren Reiseandenken, Lieblingsobjekten und Werken von Künstlern und zeitgenössischen Designern zu wandeln. Die begabte Landschaftsarchitektin May de Lasteyrie hat um das Haus einen Garten mit Buchsbaumrabatten angelegt, der von der Kindheit Carolines in Georgetown inspiriert ist.

"Cuando empezamos a buscar un lugar en el que vivir, teníamos la esperanza de descubrir un apartamento muy luminoso en París. Sin embargo, en cuanto vimos este taller artístico del siglo XIX, ¡fue amor a primera vista! Con la ayuda del arquitecto Jacques Danan, Caroline reformó completamente el taller. Gracias al enlucido de la fachada exterior, la remodelación de los suelos y los cuartos de estar y la restauración de los elementos deteriorados, el taller ha recuperado su sello de época. Caroline ha sabido darle a este lugar un encanto familiar e intemporal manteniéndose fiel a su historia y a su energía artística. Ha combinado muebles que han pertenecido a su familia durante generaciones con creaciones originales de sus artistas y artesanos favoritos. Caroline se dispuso a crear un hogar que se le asemejase, que poseyese un alma. Hoy, uno puede pasearse con deleite entre sus recuerdos de viaje, sus objetos preferidos y las obras de artistas y diseñadores contemporáneos. La casa da a un jardín de macizos de bojes diseñado por la talentosa paisajista May de Lasteyrie, que se inspiró en la infancia de Caroline en Georgetown.

"Partiti alla ricerca di una casa, della 'nostra' casa, io e mio marito sognavamo di trovare un appartamento molto luminoso nel cuore di Parigi. Ma non appena ci siamo imbattuti in questo laboratorio artistico del XIX secolo ne siamo stati immediatamente folgorati!". Con la collaborazione dell'architetto Jacques Danan, Caroline Sarkozy ha restaurato da cima a fondo l'atelier. Il ripristino della facciata esterna, il rifacimento dei pavimenti e degli spazi quotidiani, il restauro degli elementi deteriorati, tutto ha contribuito a restituire all'ambiente la sua bellezza d'epoca. Caroline ha saputo riscaldare questo luogo rivestendolo di un fascino domestico quasi sospeso nel tempo, pur restando fedele al suo passato e all'energia creativa di cui era pervaso. Ha abbinato elementi d'arredo che appartengono alla sua famiglia da generazioni alle creazioni originali degli artisti e degli artigiani che predilige. Si è impegnata a dar vita a uno spazio intimo e personale che le somigliasse, che possedesse un'anima, dove è dilettevole aggirarsi tra i suoi souvenir di viaggio, tra gli oggetti che più ama, tra le opere di artisti e designer contemporanei. La casa si apre su un giardino di cespugli di bosso progettato dall'esperta paesaggista May de Lasteyrie, che per la sua realizzazione si è ispirata all'infanzia di Caroline a Georgetown.

The living room is awash with light from the studio's large windows. The coffee table and daisy pedestal tables are by Hubert Le Gall, while the leather armchairs are by Gio Ponti, and the lamps placed on the windowsills, in the background, bear the signature of Paul Laszlo.

Dans le salon inondé de lumière grâce aux baies vitrées de l'atelier, la table basse et les guéridons marguerites sont d'Hubert Le Gall, les fauteuils anglais en cuir de Gio Ponti et les lampes posées sur les rebords des fenêtres à l'arrière-plan sont signées Paul Laszlo.

Dieser Blick in den lichtdurchfluteten Wohnraum zeigt die bleigefassten Atelierfenster, einen Couchtisch und Gänseblümchen-Beistelltische, die von Hubert Le Gall entworfen wurden, lederbezogene englische Sessel von Gio Ponti und Lampen von Paul Laszlo ihm Hintergrund auf der Fensterbank.

En el salón, inundado de luz gracias a los ventanales del taller, la mesa baja y los veladores son de Hubert Le Gall, los sillones ingleses de cuero son de Gio Ponti y las lámparas que reposan sobre las repisas de las ventanas en segundo plano son un diseño de Paul Laszlo.

Nel mare di luce che inonda il living dalle basse vetrate dell'atelier risaltano il coffee-table e i tavolini rotondi a margherita di Hubert Le Gall, le poltrone inglesi in pelle di Gio Ponti e, in secondo piano sul davanzale interno, le lampade firmate Paul Laszlo.

In the dining room, the Gio Ponti chairs are upholstered with Senegalese artist Aissa Dione fabric. The American Empire-style table previously belonged to Caroline's great-great-grandfather, John Ellis White. The books adorning the library form part of her husband's family collection. The staircase is decorated with a custom-made cotton and raffia fabric by Aissa Dione, a curved wall light in straw by Hubert Le Gall, and a Paavo Tynell chandelier.

Dans la salle à manger, les chaises signées Gio Ponti sont recouvertes d'un tissu de l'artiste sénégalaise Aissa Dione. La table de style Empire américain a jadis appartenu à sa trisaïeule John Ellis White. La collection de livres qui orne la bibliothèque fait partie de la collection familiale du mari de Caroline. L'escalier est décoré d'un tissu en coton et raphia créé pour l'occasion par Aissa Dione, d'une applique serpentin en paille d'Hubert Le Gall et d'une suspension signée Paavo Tynell.

Die Esszimmerstühle, ein Entwurf Gio Pontis, sind mit afrikanischem Stoff von der senegalesischen Designerin Aissa Dione bezogen. Der Tisch im Stil des American Empire gehörte einst Caroline Sarkozys Urgroßvater John Ellis White. Die Buchkollektion, die in der Bibliothek prunkt, ist Teil des Familienbesitzes ihres Ehemannes. Die Treppe ist mit einem speziell für diesen Anlass gefertigten Stoff aus Baumwolle und Bast von Aissa Dione bezogen, die Stroh-Wandlampe stammt von Hubert Le Gall und der Deckenleuchter von Paavo Tynell.

En el comedor, las sillas, firmadas por Gio Ponti, están cubiertas con una tela de la artista senegalesa Aissa Dione. La mesa de estilo Imperio americano perteneció en otro tiempo a su tatarabuelo John Ellis White. La colección de libros que habita la biblioteca forma parte de la colección familiar del esposo de Caroline. La escalera está decorada con una tela de algodón y rafia creada para la ocasión por Aissa Dione, un aplique serpentino de paja de Hubert Le Gall y un candelabro firmado por Paavo Tynell.

Nella sala da pranzo, le sedie firmate Gio Ponti sono rivestite con un tessuto della designer senegalese Aissa Dione. Il tavolo americano stile Impero apparteneva al trisavolo di Caroline, John Ellis White. La raccolta di libri che impreziosisce la biblioteca fa parte della collezione di famiglia del marito di Caroline. Il vano scala, rivestito con un tessuto di cotone e rafia realizzato su misura di Aissa Dione, è illuminato da lampade a parete in paglia di Hubert Le Gall e da un lampadario firmato Paavo Tynell.

Coral Reef Penthouse

Saint-Germain-des-Prés

Tino Zervudachi, with MHZ Interior Design and Decoration, remains true to David Mlinaric's legacy: the notion of understating formality by eliciting the refinement and elegance that results from transforming spaces, combining colors and textures with the aesthetics of contemporary and classic interiors. For this apartment in Saint-Germain-des-Prés, Zervudachi's goal was not only to provide a beautiful and comfortable home to his clients. He wanted to create a refined and pure backdrop to suit each object and work of art that reflects its owner's personality. The entrance opens to a magnificent staircase with zinc railings designed by Manuela Zervudachi. The living room was revisited with sober architectural interiors; the golden-hue lacquered wood fretworks give an effect of higher ceilings and light. An old map of Paris dresses the living room's ceiling while a James Brown painting hangs over a sofa also by Manuela Zervudachi. From the guest bedroom a secret hallway reveals a room filled with hidden treasures.

Avec l'agence d'architecture MHZ Interior Design and Decoration, Tino Zervudachi reste fidèle à l'héritage de David Mlinaric : sobriété formelle et évocation du raffinement et de l'élégance par la transformation des espaces, et combinaison harmonieuse des couleurs et des textures avec l'esthétique des intérieurs contemporains et classiques. Pour cet appartement situé à Saint-Germain-des-Prés, Zervudachi ne voulait pas simplement offrir une belle demeure confortable à ses clients. Il souhaitait créer une toile de fond raffinée et pure susceptible d'accueillir tous les objets et œuvres d'art reflétant la personnalité de leur propriétaire. L'entrée dévoile un magnifique escalier doté de rampes en zinc signées Manuela Zervudachi. Le salon a été revisité dans un style architectural sobre ; les éléments en bois vernis doré accentuent l'impression de hauteur sous plafond et de luminosité. Une vieille carte de Paris habille le plafond du salon, et un tableau du peintre James Brown est suspendu au-dessus du canapé, que l'on doit également à Manuela Zervudachi. Depuis la chambre d'amis, un vestibule secret nous conduit à une pièce remplie de trésors cachés.

Tino Zervudachi, Mitinhaber von MHZ Interior Design and Decoration, bleibt dem Erbe von David Mlinaric treu und somit der Idee einer zurückhaltenden Formensprache, erzielt durch raffiniert und elegant umgestaltete Räume, bei denen Farben und Texturen mit der Ästhetik zeitgenössischer und klassischer Inneneinrichtung verbunden werden. Zervudachi wollte diese Wohnung nicht nur in ein schönes und behagliches Heim für seine Kunden verwandeln, sondern auch einen edlen und unverfälschten Rahmen für die Objekte und Kunstwerke schaffen, die die Persönlichkeit ihres Besitzers widerspiegeln. Hinter dem Eingang befindet sich eine prachtvolle Treppe mit einem Geländer aus Zink, entworfen von Manuela Zervudachi. Das Wohnzimmer greift die Idee schlichter architektonischer Interieurs wieder auf; die in einem Goldton lackierten Holzornamente lassen die Decken höher und den Raum heller erscheinen. Ein alter Stadtplan von Paris ziert die Decke des Wohnzimmers, während über einem Sofa, ebenfalls von Manuela Zervudachi, ein Bild von James Brown hängt. Vom Gästebad führt ein versteckter Flur zu einem Zimmer voller verborgener Schätze.

Tino Zervudachi, junto a MHZ Interior Design and Decoration, saint se mantiene fiel al legado de David Mlinaric, la noción de entender la formalidad mediante la obtención del refinamiento y la elegancia que resultan de trasformar espacios, combinar colores y texturas con las estéticas de los interiores contemporáneos y clásicos. Para este apartamento en Staint-Germain-de-Près, la intención de Zervudachi no era sólo la de proporcionar un hogar bonito y confortable a sus clientes. Deseaba crear un telón de fondo refinado y puro para combinar cada objeto y obra de arte que reflejan la personalidad de su dueño. La entrada se abre a una magnífica escalera con barandillas de cinc diseñadas por Manuela Zervudachi. El salón fue revisado con interiores de arquitectura sobria; los calados de madera lacados en tonalidades doradas para crear un efecto de techos más altos y luminosidad. Un viejo mapa de París viste el techo del salón mientras una pintura de James Brown cuelga sobre un sofá, también de Manuela Zervudachi. Desde el dormitorio de huéspedes, un pasillo secreto descubre una habitación repleta de tesoros escondidos.

Tino Zervudachi, della MHZ Interior Design and Decoration, fedele all'insegnamento di David Mlinaric interpreta il concetto di formalità attenuata valorizzando la raffinatezza e l'eleganza che emergono dalla trasformazione degli spazi e dalla combinazione dei colori e delle texture secondo i canoni estetici degli interni classici e contemporanei. Per questo appartamento nel quartiere di Saint-Germain-des-Prés, Zervudachi non si è posto come unico fine quello di confezionare una casa bella e confortevole per i suoi clienti, ma ha voluto creare uno sfondo essenziale e raffinato che si modellasse sulla collezione di oggetti e opere d'arte in cui si riflette la personalità dei proprietari. L'ingresso si apre su una magnifica scala elicoidale con balaustra di zinco disegnata da Manuela Zervudachi. Il living è stato rivisitato con linee architettoniche sobrie, che vedono nella scelta degli ornamenti a greca, realizzati in legno laccato dalle tonalità dorate, un espediente per aumentare la verticalità dei soffitti e intensificare la luce. Una vecchia cartina di Parigi riveste il soffitto del living, dove un pannello di James Brown completa lo spazio sovrastante un sofà di Manuela Zervudachi. Dalla camera degli ospiti un vestibolo segreto rivela una stanza ricolma di tesori nascosti.

This view of the living room displays a red love seat and console by Manuela Zervudachi and coffee table by Dupré-Lafon. A marble top 18th-century Chinese lacquered commode showcases the owner's collection of corals and artwork. The dining room fuses corals with contemporary art, a De Roche crystal chandelier hovers over the table and on the Onyx mantelpiece, and the Tour de Babel sculpture by Manuela Zervudachi is flanked by coral.

Dans le salon, la causeuse rouge et la console sont de Manuela Zervudachi, la table basse de Dupré-Lafon. Une commode chinoise laquée du XVIIIᵉ siècle à dessus en marbre abrite la collection de coraux et d'œuvres d'art du propriétaire. Dans le salon, les coraux se fondent avec l'art contemporain ; un lustre en cristal de roche semble vaciller au-dessus de la table alors que le manteau de la cheminée en onyx porte une sculpture « Tour de Babel » de Manuela Zervudachi, flanquée de coraux rouges.

Dieser Blick ins Wohnzimmer zeigt ein rotes Sofa und eine Konsole von Manuela Zervudachi, Couchtisch von Dupré-Lafon. Eine lackierte, chinesische Kommode aus dem 18. Jahrhundert mit Marmorplatte dient als Ausstellungsfläche der vom Besitzer gesammelten Korallen und Kunstwerke. Im Esszimmer treffen Korallen auf zeitgenössische Kunst. Ein Kristalllüster schwebt über dem Tisch, und auf dem Kaminsims aus Onyx steht, eingerahmt von Korallenriffen, die Skulptur „Turm zu Babel" von Manuela Zervudachi.

Esta vista del salón muestra sofá de dos plazas rojo y consola de Manuela Zervudachi, mesa de café de Dupré-Lafon. Una cómoda china lacada del siglo XVIII con cubierta de mármol presenta la colección de corales y obras de arte del propietario. El comedor funde coral con arte contemporáneo, una araña de cristal de De Roche pende sobre la mesa, y encima de la cubierta de ónice la escultura "Tour de Babel" de Manuela Zervudachi está flanqueada por arrecifes de coral.

Da questa prospettiva del living emergono il rosso intenso di un divano e la console di Manuela Zervudachi; il coffee-table è di Dupré-Lafon. Sul top in marmo di un canterano del XVIII secolo in lacca cinese è esposta la collezione di coralli e oggetti d'arte del proprietario. Nella sala da pranzo il rosso dei coralli si fonde con il gusto contemporaneo degli oggetti d'arte. Un lampadario in cristallo De Roche sovrasta il tavolo e il caminetto in onice, con la scultura "Torre di Babele" di Manuela Zervudachi quale materico contrappunto alla scarlatta levità dei coralli che le fanno da cornice.

Traveling Penthouse
Jardin des Tuileries

With its imposing view of the Tuileries, architect Laurent Bourgois and project manager Laurent Minot wanted to open up this duplex rooftop flat to create open spaces with monumental bay windows that give each room a projection over the gardens. The owners are globetrotters who collect art and relics from each country they visit. The flat features an antique Chinese door that leads to a dining room with table and chairs by Le Corbusier. An old locksmith's metal door stands beneath a floating, polished industrial iron staircase with integrated bookcase. Honey-tinted timber beams from railroad tracks replaced the original traditional style parquets. For the kitchen and bathroom floors, the architects used mosaic tiles from Damascus, a reference from antiquity, with a design inspired by the dome of a provincial Roman church. All the materials play into the theme of travel and constant movement. The architectural structure showcases ethnic objects of art that come and go in time and space.

Avec sa vue majestueuse sur les Tuileries, l'architecte Laurent Bourgois avec Laurent Minot, chargé du projet à l'agence, souhaitaient ouvrir cet appartement à double terrasse en créant des espaces ouverts à baies vitrées imposantes donnant à chaque pièce une vue sur les jardins. Les propriétaires sont des globe-trotters ramenant des œuvres et des souvenirs de chaque pays qu'ils visitent. L'appartement s'ouvre par une porte chinoise ancienne sur la salle à manger avec sa table et ses chaises dessinées par Le Corbusier. L'escalier flottant en acier poli design industriel avec bibliothèque intégrée surplombe une vieille porte métallique en ferronnerie d'art. Des traverses de voie ferrée fumées couleur miel remplacent les anciens parquets traditionnels. Pour les sols de la cuisine et de la salle de bains, les architectes ont utilisé de la mosaïque de Damas, référence à l'Antiquité, avec un motif inspiré d'une coupole d'église romane de province. Tous les matériaux jouent sur le thème du voyage et du mouvement permanent. La structure architecturale met quant à elle en scène des objets d'art de cultures populaires intemporels et universels.

Der beeindruckende Ausblick auf die Tuilerien bewog den Architekten Laurent Bourgeois und den Projektleiter Laurent Minot diese sich über zwei Geschosse erstreckende Dachgeschosswohnung zu öffnen und weite Räume mit besonders großen Fensteröffnungen zu schaffen, sodass jeder Raum Blick auf die Gärten hat. Die Eigentümer sind Globetrotter, die in jedem Land, das sie besuchen, Kunstobjekte und andere Gegenstände sammeln. Durch eine antike chinesische Tür gelangt man in das mit Tisch und Stühlen von Le Corbusier ausgestatte Esszimmer. Eine alte handgeschmiedete Tür steht unter einer glänzenden freitragenden Industrie-Stahltreppe mit integriertem Bücherregal. Die ursprünglichen klassischen Parkettböden wurden durch honigfarbene Eisenbahn-Holzbohlen ersetzt. In den Fußböden von Küche und Bad verarbeiteten die Architekten Mosaike aus Damaskus als Anspielung auf die Antike, deren Entwurf von der Kuppel einer romanischen Kirche inspiriert ist. Alle Materialien spielen auf das Thema des Reisens und des konstanten In-Bewegung-Seins an. Die Architektur schafft hier einen Rahmen für zeitlose und universelle Kunstobjekte.

Con sus impresionantes vistas del jardín de las Tullerías, el arquitecto Laurent Bourgois y Laurent Minot, gestor del proyecto, deseaban construir este adosado en el ático con el fin de crear espacios amplios con ventanas monumentales que dan a cada habitación proyección a los jardines. Los propietarios son trotamundos que coleccionan piezas de arte y reliquias de cada país que visitan. El apartamento presenta una antigua puerta china que lleva a un comedor con mesa y sillas de Le Corbusier. Una vieja puerta metálica de cerrajero se levanta bajo unas escaleras flotantes de hierro industrial pulido, con estantería de libros encastrada. Vigas de madera de color miel, sacadas de vías de tren, sustituyeron a los parqués originales de estilo tradicional. Para los suelos de la cocina y el baño, los arquitectos utilizaron mosaico de Damasco, una referencia de la antigüedad, de diseño inspirado en la cúpula de una iglesia provincial romana. Todos los materiales siguen la temática de los viajes y el movimiento constante, la estructura arquitectónica exhibe objetos étnicos de arte que vienen y van en el tiempo y el espacio.

Forte dell'imponente veduta delle Tuileries, l'architetto Laurent Bourgois, in collaborazione con Laurent Minot, responsabile dei lavori, ha voluto dilatare questo appartamento in duplex all'ultimo piano per creare ampi spazi dotati di monumentali finestre a bovindo che consentissero la vista sui giardini da ogni stanza. I proprietari sono irriducibili giramondo che collezionano oggetti d'arte e souvenir di ogni Paese che visitano. L'appartamento è caratterizzato da un'antica porta cinese che immette in una sala da pranzo arredata con tavolo e sedie di Le Corbusier. Una vecchia porta di metallo lavorato si delinea sotto una scala di ferro industriale dalle linee pulite con libreria integrata. Vecchie traversine ferroviarie di legno color miele hanno sostituito il classico parquet originale. Per i pavimenti di bagno e cucina gli architetti ha utilizzato mosaici Damasco, un richiamo all'antichità ispirato alla cupola di una chiesa di una provincia romana. Tutti i materiali giocano sul tema del viaggio e del perenne movimento, con la scaffalatura d'autore quale vetrina di oggetti d'arte etnica che fluttuano nel tempo e nello spazio.

The dining room table and chairs by Le Corbusier were found in a library in Gujarat.

Création de Le Corbusier, la table et les chaises du salon proviennent d'une bibliothèque du Gujarat.

Der Esstisch und die Stühle von Le Corbusier stammen aus einer Bibliothek in Gujarat.

La mesa del comedor y las sillas de Le Corbusier fueron halladas en una biblioteca de Gujarat.

Il tavolo e le sedie di Le Corbusier della sala da pranzo provengono da una biblioteca del Gujarat.

The bathroom features mosaic floors from Damascus, and antique mirrors frame a porcelain 1930s bathtub.

La salle de bains permet d'admirer des sols en mosaïque de Damas et une baignoire en porcelaine années 1930 cernée d'anciens miroirs.

Fußbodenmosaike aus Damaskus schmücken das Badezimmer und antike Spiegel rahmen die Porzellanbadewanne aus den 1930er Jahren.

El baño tiene suelos con mosaicos de Damasco y espejos antiguos que enmarcan una bañera de porcelana de los años 30.

Nel bagno spiccano pavimenti decorati con mosaici Damasco e specchi antichi che inquadrano la vasca in porcellana anni '30.

East Meets West

Palais-Royal

Singapore-based designer Christopher Noto brings the East to the City of Lights. His rue de Richelieu *pied-à-terre* is a dream come true from his earlier years as a student in Paris. Inspired by its surroundings near the Palais-Royal and Tuileries, he wanted to pay tribute to quintessential France with a touch of Asia's aesthetic richness. He used a palette of warm colors and harmonizing tones to bring out the textures, moldings and wrought-iron balustrades. Baby powder and Japanese varnish was used to metamorphose the yellow-toned herringbone wooden floors to a sea of silvery blue parquetry. Ming Dynasty fretwork panels fit perfectly within the wall's paneling and his collection of Asian art, ranging from Ming and early Qing Dynasty furniture—stone Foo Dogs to samurai paintings by Christian de Laubadère—all become one with Jaya Ibrahim-designed sofa and French 18th–19th-century furnishings. Noto transformed the kitchen into a bath with a functioning fireplace, 18th-century marble floors and a Louis XVI fauteuil that makes the room look more like a *fumoir* than a bath.

Installé à Singapour, le designer Christopher Noto apporte une note orientale à la Ville Lumière. Son pied-à-terre rue de Richelieu est la concrétisation d'un rêve imaginé à ses débuts à Paris en tant qu'étudiant. Inspiré par son cadre de vie, entre le Palais-Royal et les Tuileries, il veut rendre hommage à l'identité française tout en évoquant en filigrane la richesse esthétique de l'Asie. Utilisant une palette de couleurs chaudes et de teintes harmonieuses, il fait ressortir les textures, les moulures et les balustrades en fer forgé. Du talc et du vernis japonais transforment les parquets de bois à chevrons cuivrés en océan gris argent. Les panneaux chantournés Ming s'intègrent parfaitement aux lambris. Avec sa collection d'art asiatique, depuis les meubles de la dynastie Ming et du début de la dynastie Qing, les chiens de Fô en pierre et le tableau de samouraï par Christian de Laubadère, l'ensemble se fond avec le canapé dessiné par Jaya Ibrahim et les meubles XVIIIᵉ et XIXᵉ. Noto a transformé la cuisine en salle de bains, avec une cheminée en état de marche ; les dalles de marbre XVIIIᵉ et le fauteuil Louis XVI font plus ressembler la pièce à un fumoir qu'à une salle de bains.

Der in Singapur lebende Designer Christopher Noto holt Fernost in die Stadt der Lichter. Sein *pied-à-terre* in der Rue de Richelieu ist ein wahr gewordener Traum seiner Pariser Studentenzeit. Inspiriert von der Umgebung, nahe des Palais-Royal und der Tuilerien, schuf er eine Hommage an den urfranzösischen Wohnstil mit einer Nuance des asiatisch-ästhetischen Reichtums. Er setzte warme Farben und harmonisierende Töne ein, um Texturen, Stuck und gusseiserne Balustraden hervorzuheben. Mit Babypuder und japanischem Lack verwandelte er das gelbe Fischgrätmuster des Holzbodens in ein Meer silbrig-blauen Parketts. Geschnitzte Holzpaneele aus der Ming-Dynastie fügen sich perfekt in die Wandgestaltung ein, und seine asiatische Kunstsammlung, die Mobiliar aus der Ming- und frühen Qing-Dynastie, steinerne Fu-Hunde und Samuraibilder von Christian de Laubadère umfasst, bildet eine Einheit mit dem von Jaya Ibrahim entworfenen Sofa und französischen Möbeln des 18. und 19. Jahrhunderts. Noto machte aus der Küche ein Bad mit funktionstüchtigem Kamin, Marmorböden des 18. Jahrhunderts und einem Louis-seize-Sessel, wodurch der Raum eher wie ein *fumoir* als ein Badezimmer aussieht.

El diseñador Christopher Noto, afincado en Singapur, trae Oriente a la Ciudad de las Luces. Con su *pied-à-terre* en la Rue de Richelieu hizo realidad un sueño de sus años como estudiante en París. Inspirado por los alrededores, cerca del Palais-Royal y el jardín de las Tullerías, deseaba rendir tributo a la esencia de Francia con un toque de la riqueza estética asiática. Utilizó una paleta de colores cálidos, armonizando tonos para resaltar las texturas, los moldes y las balaustradas de hierro forjado. Se empleó talco para bebés y barniz japonés para metamorfosear los suelos de madera en espiga de tonos amarillentos en un mar de parqué azul plateado. Los paneles calados de la Dinastía Ming se ajustan perfectamente dentro de los paneles de las paredes y su colección de arte asiático, que va desde mobiliario de la Dinastía Ming y comienzos de la Qing, pasando por perros foo de piedra, hasta pinturas samuráis de Christian de Laubadère, todo conjuntado con sofás diseñados por Jaya Ibrahim y muebles franceses de los siglos XVIII y XIX. Noto transformó la cocina en un baño con chimenea propia, suelos de mármol del siglo XVIII y un sillón Luis XVI que hacen que la habitación parezca más una sala para fumar que un baño.

Oggi di stanza a Singapore, il designer Christopher Noto ha portato l'Oriente nella Ville Lumière. Il *pied-à-terre* in rue de Richelieu è la materializzazione di un sogno iniziato durante i primi anni della sua carriera di studente a Parigi, quando viveva nei pressi del Palais-Royal e delle Tuileries. Ispirandosi all'atmosfera del suo quartiere, ha voluto rendere omaggio alla Francia più autentica con un tocco di ricchezza estetica orientale, utilizzando una tavolozza di colori caldi e tonalità armoniche che dessero risalto alle texture, agli stucchi e alle balaustre in ferro battuto. Talco e lacca giapponese hanno trasformato i pavimenti in legno a spina di pesce color miele in un mare di parquet azzurro-argento. I pannelli traforati di epoca Ming si inseriscono perfettamente tra le pannellature delle pareti e la collezione d'arte orientale di Noto, che spazia dai mobili di epoca Ming e della prima dinastia Qing, ai cani guardiani in pietra, fino ai ritratti di samurai di Christian de Laubadère, tutti a formare un unico insieme con il divano di Jaya Ibrahim e il mobilio del XVIII e XIX francese. Noto ha poi trasformato la cucina in un bagno, completo di caminetto funzionante, pavimento in marmo del XVIII secolo e una poltrona Luigi XVI che rende l'ambiente più simile a quello di un *fumoir*.

The bedroom and bathroom display traditional fireplaces and Louis XVI furnishings in raw linens. A fossilized tree trunk pedestal table stands in front of the bathtub.

Dans la chambre et la salle de bains, on peut admirer des cheminées à l'ancienne et des meubles Louis XVI tendus de lin naturel. Devant la baignoire, une souche d'arbre fossilisée fait office de guéridon.

In Badezimmer und Schlafraum prunken klassische Kamine und mit Rohleinen bezogene Louis-seize-Möbel. Vor der Badewanne steht ein Tisch aus einem versteinerten Baumstamm.

Dormitorio y baño presentan chimeneas tradicionales y muebles Luis XVI en lino en bruto. Frente a la bañera se encuentra un velador que es un tronco de árbol fosilizado.

La camera da letto e il bagno presentano caminetti tradizionali e mobili Luigi XVI rivestiti con lini grezzi. Un tronco fossile fa le veci di un tavolino di servizio accanto alla vasca.

The dining area with its curved wall creates a niche for furnishings by Jaya Ibrahim. A second Christian de Laubadère painting graces the wall above an Empire style sofa with cushions and curtains designed by Jim Thompson and Rubelli.

Avec ses murs aux lignes courbes, la salle à manger forme comme une niche pour les meubles de Jaya Ibrahim. Dans la pièce tendue de rideaux Rubelli, un second tableau de Christian de Laubadère agrémente le mur au-dessus du canapé style Empire orné de coussins de Jim Thompson.

Das Esszimmer mit seiner geschwungenen Fassade bildet eine Nische für Jaya Ibrahim-Möbel. Ein zweites Gemälde von Christian de Laubadère ziert die Wand über dem Empire-Stil-Sofa; Kissen und Gardinen sind Entwürfe von Jim Thompson und Rubelli.

La zona de almuerzo con su pared curva crea un nicho para los muebles de Jaya Ibrahim. Una segunda pintura de Christian de Laubadère embellece la pared sobre un sofá de estilo imperial, con cojines y cortinas diseñadas por Jim Thompson y Rubelli.

Nella zona pranzo la parete smussata crea una nicchia per i mobili di Jaya Ibrahim. Un secondo dipinto di Christian de Laubadère ingentilisce la parete sopra il sofà stile impero con cuscini e tendaggi di Jim Thompson e Rubelli.

Poetic Justice

Palais-Royal

When renowned interior designer Jacques Grange first acquired the apartment in the Palais-Royal that once was home to the novelist Colette, he filled every space with profusion of her works and relics. Colette's haven overlooking the gardens has undergone several transformations ever since. His latest renovation was intent on reconciling the apartment's 18th-century architectural lines with the Palais Royal. It has become a showcase—an homage to everything he loves. A collector's home inhabited by his favorite paintings, sculptures and furnishings from the 18th to 20th century, all pulled together harmoniously by a strong sense of personality. The entrance offers a soothing effect with a Sugimoto photo sharing space with a neoclassic 18th-century Lucca bust wearing an Amazonian feather headpiece. An explosive Damien Hirst painting dominates the main wall of the antechamber and the dining room has an immense skylight Grange designed in Cubist style with an Arts and Crafts Movement lantern by Greene & Greene circa 1900.

Lorsqu'il fait l'acquisition de cet appartement autrefois propriété de Colette, le célèbre décorateur Jacques Grange remplit tout de suite l'espace de nombre de ses œuvres et souvenirs. Situé dans les jardins du Palais-Royal, l'ancien refuge de la romancière a subi depuis de nombreuses transformations. La dernière rénovation était destinée à harmoniser les lignes architecturales XVIIIe siècle de l'appartement avec celles du Palais-Royal. C'est devenu une vitrine, un hommage à tout ce qu'aime Grange : une maison de collectionneur habitée par ses tableaux, sculptures et meubles préférés du XVIIIe au XXe siècle, harmonieusement agencés et reflétant fortement la personnalité de leur propriétaire. L'entrée produit un effet apaisant grâce à la photographie de Sugimoto qui partage l'espace avec un buste néoclassique XVIIIe de Lucca, arborant une coiffe amazonienne. Un tableau de Damien Hirst domine le mur principal de l'antichambre. Dans le salon, une immense lucarne dessinée par Grange en style cubiste côtoie une lanterne du mouvement Arts and Crafts dessinée par l'agence d'architecture Greene and Greene vers 1900.

Als der bekannte Innenarchitekt Jacques Grange die Wohnung, in der einst die Schriftstellerin Colette gelebt hatte, erwarb, bestückte er zunächst jeden Raum verschwenderisch mit ihren Arbeiten und Andenken. Seitdem hat er Colettes Zufluchtsort in den Gärten des Palais-Royal mehrmals umgestaltet. Mit der letzten Renovierung beabsichtigte er, die architektonische Linienführung der Wohnung aus dem 18. Jahrhundert mit der des Palais Royal in Einklang zu bringen. Das Apartment hat sich zu einem Ausstellungsraum entwickelt, einer Hommage an alles, was er liebt und schätzt. Es ist unverkennbar der Ort, an dem ein Sammler wohnt, wo seine Lieblingsstücke, Gemälde, Skulpturen und Mobiliar des 18. bis 20. Jahrhunderts zu Hause sind, harmonisch und mit feinem Gespür für Individualität zusammengestellt. Der Eingangsbereich wirkt beruhigend mit einem Foto von Sugimoto, das sich den Raum mit einer neoklassischen Lucca-Büste aus dem 18. Jahrhundert teilt, die einen Federschmuck vom Amazonas trägt. Ein explosives Gemälde von Damien Hirst beherrscht die Wand im Vestibül. Den Speisesaal schmückt ein großes, von Grange im kubistischen Stil entworfenes Oberlicht und eine Lampe von Greene and Greene im Stil der Arts-and-Crafts-Bewegung, um 1900.

Cuando el renombrado diseñador de interiores Jacques Grange adquirió el apartamento que en su día fue el hogar de la novelista Colette, llenó cada espacio con multitud de trabajos y reliquias de la escritora. El refugio de Colette en los jardines del Palais-Royal ha sufrido varias transformaciones desde entonces. Su última renovación fue un intento de reconciliar las líneas arquitectónicas del apartamento, del siglo XVIII, con el Palais Royal. Se ha convertido en un escaparate, un homenaje a todo lo que él ama. La casa de un coleccionista habitada por sus pinturas, esculturas y muebles favoritos del periodo comprendido entre los siglos XVIII y XX, todos dispuestos de forma armoniosa con un gran sentido de la personalidad. La entrada transmite un efecto relajante, con una foto de Sugimoto compartiendo espacio con un busto neoclásico de Lucca del siglo XVIII, el cual porta una corona con plumas de la selva amazónica. Una explosiva pintura de Damien Hirst domina la pared principal de la antecámara y el comedor cuenta con un inmenso tragaluz diseñado por el propio Grange en estilo cubista, además de una lámpara del movimiento Arts and Crafts de Greene and Greene, aproximadamente de 1900.

Quando il celebre architetto d'interni Jacques Grange acquistò l'appartamento che un tempo fu di Colette, ne riempì ogni spazio con una profusione di opere e oggetti legati alla grande scrittrice francese. Da allora, il paradiso di Colette incorniciato dai giardini del Palais-Royal ha subito numerose trasformazioni. L'intervento più recente ha voluto riconciliare le linee architettoniche settecentesche dell'abitazione con lo storico Palais Royal. Grange ne ha fatto una vetrina, un omaggio a tutto ciò che egli ama di più. È la casa di un collezionista dove dimorano i quadri, le sculture, i mobili che egli predilige, pezzi di un periodo compreso tra il XVIII il XX secolo che convivono armoniosamente grazie a uno spiccato senso della personalità. L'ingresso è pervaso dall'effetto lenitivo di uno scatto di Sugimoto, che condivide lo spazio con un busto neoclassico settecentesco di Lucca cinto da un copricapo amazzone piumato. Un esplosivo pannello di Damien Hirst domina la parete principale dell'anticamera e dall'ampio lucernario che copre la sala da pranzo, progettato da Grange in stile cubista, scende una lanterna Arts & Crafts di Greene e Greene (1900 circa).

View from the master bedroom that opens up to the gardens of the Palais-Royal.

Vue depuis la chambre de maître donnant sur les jardins du Palais-Royal.

Blick aus dem Hauptschlafzimmer, das auf die Gärten des Palais-Royal hinausgeht.

Vista del dormitorio principal que se abre a los jardines del Palais-Royal.

Vista dalla camera padronale sui giardini del Palais-Royal.

A portrait of Colette by Irving Penn overlooking a bronze bust of herself by Fenosa. On the fireplace a Janniot 1920s alabaster bust wearing a feather Amazonian headpiece and 19th-century chaise longue exactly where Colette had hers.

Le portrait de Colette par Irving Penn toise le buste en bronze de la romancière par Fenosa. Sur la cheminée, un buste en albâtre de Janniot des années 1920 arbore une coiffe d'Amazonie, tandis que la chaise longue du XIXe demeure à la même place qu'à l'époque de Colette.

Ein Portrait Colettes von Irving Penn blickt auf eine bronzene Büste von Fenosa, die sie darstellt. Auf dem Kaminsims steht eine Alabasterbüste von Janniot aus den 1920er Jahren, die einen Federschmuck vom Amazonas trägt, und die Chaiselongue aus dem 19. Jahrhundert steht genau dort, wo die von Colette stand.

Retrato de Colette de Irving Penn con la vista sobre un busto de bronce de ella misma realizado por Fenosa. En la chimenea, un busto de alabastro de Janniot años 20 que porta una corona con plumas de la selva amazónica y una tumbona del siglo XIX, exactamente donde Colette tenía la suya.

Realizzato da Irving Penn, un ritratto di Colette spicca dietro a un busto in bronzo di Fenosa, anch'esso ispirato alla scrittrice. Sul caminetto un busto in alabastro di Janniot degli anni '20 cinto da un copricapo amazzone piumato e, vicino, una chaise longue del XIX secolo posta esattamente dove Colette teneva la sua.

In the entrance hallway, a François-Xavier Lalanne sculpture stands in front of an object by Daniel Buren. The dining room displays a painting by Pierre Lesieur and a Harry Bertoia bronze.

Dans le couloir de l'entrée, une sculpture de François-Xavier Lalanne fait face à une œuvre de Daniel Buren. Dans la salle à manger, on peut admirer des tableaux de Pierre Lesieur et un bronze d'Harry Bertoia.

Im Eingangsflur steht eine Skulptur von François-Xavier Lalanne vor einem Objekt von Daniel Buren. Der Speisesaal stellt Gemälde von Pierre Lesieur und eine Bronzestatue von Harry Bertoia aus.

En el pasillo de entrada, una escultura de François-Xavier Lalanne se alza frente a un objeto de Daniel Buren. El comedor contiene pinturas de Pierre Lesieur y una escultura de bronce de Harry Bertoia.

Nel corridoio d'ingresso, una scultura di François-Xavier Lalanne risalta di fronte a un oggetto di Daniel Buren. Nella sala da pranzo si distinguono un quadro di Pierre Lesieur e un bronzo di Harry Bertoia.

The chandelier in the bathroom is a confection of gilt fern fronds that once belonged to Madeleine Castaing; against the wall stands a Louise Bourgeois porcelain sculpture. In the master bedroom, a Boiceau carpet is draped over a 19th-century brass bed.

Composé de frondes de fougères dorées, le lustre de la salle de bains appartenait autrefois à Madeleine Castaing ; au mur est adossée une sculpture en porcelaine de Louise Bourgeois. Dans la chambre de maître, un tapis Boiceau est tendu au-dessus d'un lit en laiton du XIXe.

Der Kerzenleuchter im Bad, der einst im Besitz von Madeleine Castaing war, wurde aus vergoldeten Farnwedeln hergestellt; an der Wand steht eine Porzellanskulptur von Louise Bourgeois. Im Hauptschlafzimmer ist ein Boiceau-Teppich über einem Messingbett aus dem 19. Jahrhundert drapiert.

La araña de luces del baño es una confección de frondas de helechos dorados que una vez perteneció a Madeleine Castaing; contra la pared se alza una escultura de porcelana de Louise Bourgeois. En el dormitorio principal, una alfombra de Boiceau yace sobre una cama de latón del siglo XIX.

Il lampadario del bagno è un intreccio di foglie di felce dorate appartenuto a Madeleine Castaing; contro il muro è addossata una scultura in porcellana di Louise Bourgeois. Nella camera padronale, un tappeto Boiceau è appeso sopra un letto in ottone del XIX secolo.

Avant-garde Rocks
Saint-Germain-des-Prés

A friendship was born from a shared passion for 20th-century art and avant-garde design from the 1940s to the 1970s. What this collector discovered when he walked into Yves Gastou's gallery on rue Bonaparte was the peak of his fervor for an almost forgotten generation of talented artists and designers. Gastou helped materialize his dream by creating a universe that showcases the wealth of playful, carefree styles of the 1940s through the 1970s with its unique mixture of colors and materials of resin, brass, stainless steel, leather, and stone geodes. In the entrance, one is received by a quirky Gilbert and George painting, a polished aluminum sofa by Ron Arad flanked by a pair of Gilbert Poillerat mirror obelisks, and a skull sculpture which sits on a metal coffee table by Ado Chale. A Venetian crystal chandelier by Arbies hangs harmoniously over this extraordinary ensemble. Like a rolling stone that travels through time and space, their joint effort results in a celebration of the freedom and relaxed lifestyle of each decade.

Une amitié est née d'une passion commune pour l'art du XXᵉ siècle et le design avant-gardiste des années 1940 à 1970. En pénétrant dans la galerie d'Yves Gastou rue Bonaparte, ce collectionneur se découvre une ferveur extrême pour une génération presque oubliée d'artistes et de designers de talent. Gastou l'aide à concrétiser son rêve en créant un univers qui met en valeur la richesse des styles ludiques et insouciants des années 1940 à 1970, avec une association unique de couleurs et de matériaux, tels que résine, cuivre, acier inox, cuivre et géodes minérales. Dans l'entrée, on est accueilli par un tableau excentrique de Gilbert et George, un canapé en aluminium poli de Ron Arad, flanqué d'une paire d'obélisques en miroir de Gilbert Poillerat et par un crâne sculpté posé sur une table basse métallique d'Ado Chale. Un lustre vénitien en cristal d'Arbies couronne harmonieusement cet ensemble. Comme une pierre qui roule à travers le temps et l'espace, leurs efforts conjoints exaltent la liberté et le style de vie décontracté des différentes décennies.

Aus der gemeinsamen Passion für die Kunst des 20. Jahrhunderts und avantgardistisches Design der 1940er bis 1970er Jahre entwickelte sich eine Freundschaft. Als der Sammler die Galerie Yves Gastous in der Rue Bonaparte betrat, erblickte er den Gipfel seiner Leidenschaft für eine nahezu in Vergessenheit geratene Generation talentierter Künstler und Designer. Gastou half ihm seinen Traum zu verwirklichen und ein Universum zu schaffen, das den Reichtum der verspielten, sorglosen Stile der 1940er bis 1970er Jahre, mit ihren einzigartigen Farb- und Materialkombinationen, wie Kunstharz, Messing, Edelstahl, Leder und Drusen zur Schau stellt. Am Eingang wird man von einem skurrilen Gilbert and George-Gemälde und einem Ron Arad-Sofa aus glänzendem Aluminium empfangen, das von zwei Spiegelobelisken von Gilbert Poillerat und einer Schädel-Skulptur auf einem metallenen Couchtisch von Ado Chale flankiert wird. Ein venezianischer Kristalllüster von Arbies hängt ganz selbstverständlich über diesem außerordentlichen Ensemble. Es scheint wie eine rastlose Reise durch Zeit und Raum, und ihre vereinten Kräfte feiern die Freiheit und den relaxten Lebensstil jener Jahrzehnte.

La pasión compartida por el arte del siglo XX y el diseño avant-garde de los 40 y los 70 forjó una amistad. Lo que este coleccionista descubrió cuando entró en la galería de Yves Gastou en la rue Bonaparte fue la cumbre de su fervor por una casi olvidada generación de talentosos artistas y diseñadores. Gastou ayudó a materializar su sueño mediante la creación de un universo que exhibe la salud de los estilos juguetones y despreocupados de los años 40 a los 70, con su mezcla única de colores y materiales como resina, latón, acero inoxidable, cuero y geodas de piedra. En la entrada, uno es recibido por una original pintura de Gilbert and George, un sofá de aluminio pulido de Ron Arad flanqueado por un par de obeliscos de espejo de Gilbert Poillerat y una escultura con forma de cráneo sobre una mesita de café de Ado Chale. Una araña de luces de cristal veneciano de Arbies cuelga armoniosamente sobre este maravilloso elenco. Como un nómada que viaja a través del tiempo y el espacio, su esfuerzo conjunto tiene como resultado una celebración del estilo de vida libre y relajado de cada década.

Da una passione condivisa per l'arte del XX secolo e il design d'avanguardia degli anni tra il '40 e il '70 è nata un'amicizia. Quel che ha scoperto questo collezionista nella galleria di Yves Gastou in rue Bonaparte è stata l'espressione più elevata del suo entusiasmo per una generazione quasi dimenticata di artisti e designer di talento. Gastou lo ha aiutato a dar forma ai propri sogni creando un universo che riassume la ricchezza degli stili giocosi e spensierati che hanno caratterizzato il periodo tra i '40 e i '70, con la sua peculiare propensione alla mescolanza di colori e materiali, tra cui resine, ottone, acciaio inossidabile, cuoio e geodi. Un curioso pannello di Gilbert and George condivide lo spazio dell'ingresso con un divano in alluminio di Ron Arad fiancheggiato da una coppia di obelischi a specchio di Gilbert Poillerat, e con una scultura a teschio posata su un tavolino metallico di Ado Chale. Un lampadario in cristallo veneziano di Arbies sovrasta armoniosamente questo straordinario insieme. Come una trottola che viaggia sulle ali del tempo e dello spazio, lo sforzo congiunto di questi artisti erompe in un inno alla libertà e alla spensieratezza di ogni singolo periodo artistico rappresentato.

Lime green upholstered 18th-century chairs surround a Marie-Claude de Fouquieres cracked resin dining room table. What appears to be a metal sculpture feminine in form is a lamp designed by Philippe Hiquily. A perspective of the living room features a Philippe Pasqua photo over a Paul Evans console with a Robert Couturier bronze sculpture standing on the left-hand side.

Des fauteuils XVIIIe tendus de vert citron entourent une table de salle à manger en résine de polyester éclaté de Marie-Claude de Fouquieres. La sculpture aux formes féminines est en fait une lampe du créateur Philippe Hiquily. Dans le salon, on aperçoit une photo de Philippe Pasqua sur une table console de Paul Evans, avec un bronze de Robert Couturier sur la gauche.

Limonengrün gepolsterte Stühle des 18. Jahrhunderts gruppieren sich um einen rissigen Kunstharz-Esstisch von Marie-Claude de Fouquieres. Das, was so aussieht wie eine metallene Frauenskulptur entpuppt sich als Lampenentwurf von Philippe Hiquily. Dieser Blick in das Wohnzimmer zeigt ein Foto von Philippe Pasqua über einem niedrigen Paul Evans-Wandschrank neben dem links eine Bronzeskulptur von Robert Couturier steht.

Sillas del siglo XVIII tapizadas en color verde lima rodean una mesa de comedor de resina agrietada de Marie-Claude de Fouquieres. Lo que parece ser una escultura de metal con forma femenina es una lámpara diseñada por Philippe Hiquily. Una perspectiva del salón muestra una foto de Philippe Pasqua sobre una consola de Paul Evans, con una escultura de bronce de Robert Couturier en la parte izquierda.

Sedie settecentesche con tappezzeria color verde acido cingono il tavolo della sala da pranzo in resina screziata di Marie-Claude de Fouquieres. La scultura in metallo dalla sagoma femminile è in realtà una lampada disegnata da Philippe Hiquily. In una prospettiva del soggiorno risalta una fotografia di Philippe Pasqua appesa sopra una consolle di Paul Evans, con una scultura in bronzo di Robert Couturier sul lato sinistro.

This architectural bookcase houses a canny collection of primitive art. Crystal vases by Carlo Scarpa and 18ᵗʰ-century Chinese carafes decorate the console. The bedroom is dressed in tones of mauve and pink with Venetian crystal wall lamps and a chandelier circa 1940s. The leather, gold-gilded, marble top dresser is a Gilbert Poillerat creation.

Cet élément de rangement architectural abrite une collection recherchée d'art primitif. Des vases de Carlo Scarpa et des carafes chinoises du XVIIIᵉ siècle ornent la table console. La chambre habillée de tons mauves et roses est éclairée par des appliques en cristal de Venise à chandeliers années 1940. Le guéridon à double plateau cuir et marbre partiellement doré est une création de Gilbert Poillerat.

In diesem Designer-Regal ist eine mit Umsicht zusammengestellte Sammlung primitiver Kunst untergebracht. Kristallvasen von Carlo Scarpa und chinesische Karaffen aus dem 18. Jahrhundert zieren den Wandschrank. Das Schlafzimmer mit venezianischen Kristallwandlüstern und Kronleuchter, um 1940, ist in Malve und Rosa gehalten. Die vergoldete, lederbezogene Kommode mit Marmorplatte ist eine Werk Gilbert Poillerats.

Esta estantería arquitectónica contiene una refinada colección de arte primitivo. Floreros de cristal de Carlo Scarpa y garrafas chinas del siglo XVIII decoran la consola. El dormitorio está vestido con tonos malva y rosa, con lámparas de pared de cristal veneciano y araña de luces de 1940 aproximadamente. El tocador de cuero, con detalles en oro y cubierta de mármol, es una creación de Gilbert Poillerat.

Questa scaffalatura d'autore ospita un'austera collezione di arte primitiva. Vasi di cristallo firmati Carlo Scarpa e caraffe cinesi del XVIII secolo guarniscono la consolle. La camera da letto è decorata con toni malva e rosa, lampade a muro e lampadario in cristallo veneziano degli anni '40 circa. La cassettiera con finiture in cuoio, dorature e piano in marmo è un pezzo di Gilbert Poillerat.

Park Avenue in Paris

Invalides

Renowned architect and interior designer Alberto Pinto works with his clients as if he is writing a screenplay, drawing from their true stories the elements he needs to build their homes. He is anti-style; he mixes all the codes of décor and art, creating a hybrid with a French touch. For this mansion, he confected a Park Avenue style space where he could devise a cozy showcase for the collection of eclectic decorative pieces. He covered the walls with mother-of-pearl tones to spotlight the objects he exposes with love and pride. When you enter the office, there are two drawings by Alexander Calder hanging over an impressive crocodile console by François-Xavier Lalanne with an early 20th-century American lamp and an André Arbus bronze sculpture standing nearby. He is true to the notion of deconstructing styles and creating a colorful universe to emphasize the eclectic collection of artwork presented here.

Architecte d'intérieur et décorateur célèbre, Alberto Pinto travaille pour ses clients comme s'il écrivait un scénario et tirait de l'histoire de leur vie les éléments dont il a besoin pour construire leurs demeures. Opposé au style, il mélange tous les codes de la décoration et de l'art pour créer un hybride à l'esprit français. Pour cet hôtel particulier, il a créé un espace de style Park Avenue où il a pu forger un bel écrin pour une collection de pièces ornementales éclectiques. Pour les murs, il a choisi des teintes nacrées afin de faire ressortir les objets exposés avec amour et fierté. En entrant dans le bureau, on aperçoit deux dessins d'Alexander Calder toisant une impressionnante console crocodile de François-Xavier Lalanne. Sur cette dernière repose une lampe américaine du début du XXe siècle. Un bronze d'André Arbus se dresse tout près. Fidèle au concept de déconstruction des styles, Pinto s'est attaché à créer un univers biggaré mettant en valeur l'éclectisme de la collection d'œuvres d'art présentes.

Der bekannte Architekt und Innenarchitekt Alberto Pinto arbeitet mit seinen Kunden, als würde er ein Theaterstück schreiben und entnimmt ihren Lebensgeschichten die Elemente, die er braucht, um ihr Zuhause einzurichten. Sein Anti-Stil vermengt sämtliche Codes der Innenarchitektur und Kunst miteinander und schafft eine Mischform mit einem französischen Touch. Das Interieur dieser Stadvilla richtete er im Stil der Park Avenue ein und schuf eine intime Ausstellungsfläche für die Sammlung unterschiedlichster Dekorationsobjekte. Er strich die Wände in Perlmutttönen, um die liebevoll und stolz vorgeführten Ausstellungsstücke in den Mittelpunkt zu rücken. Im Arbeitszimmer erblickt man zwei Bilder Alexander Calders, die über einer imposanten Krokodilkonsole von François-Xavier Lalanne hängen. Auf der Konsole steht eine amerikanische Lampe aus dem frühen 20. Jahrhundert und daneben eine Bronzeskulptur von André Arbus. Er bleibt seiner Idee, Stile zu dekonstruieren, treu und schafft ein farbenfrohes Universum, in dem die Sammlung eklektischer Kunstobjekte gut zur Geltung kommt.

El renombrado arquitecto y diseñador de interiores Alberto Pinto trabaja con sus clientes como si estuviera escribiendo un guión, dibujando a partir de sus verdaderas historias los elementos que necesita para construir sus casas. Él es anti-estilo; mezcla todos los códigos del escenario y del arte y crea así un híbrido con un toque francés. Para esta mansión, Pinto confeccionó un espacio estilo Park Avenue en el que podía idear un acogedor escaparate para la amplia colección de piezas decorativas. Cubrió los muros con tonos madreperla para resaltar los objetos que expone con amor y orgullo. Al entrar en la oficina, se observan dos dibujos de Alexander Calder colgando sobre una impresionante consola de cocodrilo de François-Xavier Lalanne con una lámpara americana de principios del siglo XX y una escultura de bronce de André Arbus que se alza a su lado. Pinto es fiel a la noción de deconstruir de estilos y crear un universo idóneo para exhibir la ecléctica colección.

L'affermato architetto e arredatore Alberto Pinto lavora per i suoi clienti come se dovesse scriverne una dettagliata biografia, attingendo da ogni storia personale tutti gli elementi che ritiene necessari per imbastire il progetto delle loro abitazioni. Refrattario agli stili univoci, stempera l'intera gamma dei codici artistici e decorativi in un'inedita cifra stilistica venata di gusto francese. Per questa dimora ha confezionato un ambiente alla Park Avenue che fungesse anche da vetrina per l'ampia collezione di oggetti d'arredo. Ne ha rivestito le pareti con tonalità madreperlate che mettessero in risalto i pezzi che più ama esporre. Nell'ingresso, due disegni di Alexander Calder risaltano sopra una sorprendente console con top di coccodrillo di François-Xavier Lalanne su cui poggia una lampada americana d'inizio del XIX secolo, mentre una scultura in bronzo di André Arbus riempie l'angolo adiacente. Fedele al concetto di decostruzione degli stili, Pinto traccia i contorni di un universo che diventa la cornice ideale del poliedrico campionario di meraviglie.

The living room gathers every possible style of furniture and decorative pieces from each period and every part of the world. This view displays an 18th-century lacquered folding screen behind a blue satin sofa and a coffee table by Ado Chale.

Le salon réunit tous les styles possibles de mobiliers et d'éléments décoratifs de toutes les périodes et toutes les régions du monde. Le paravent laqué du XVIIIe siècle enchâsse un canapé en satin bleu et une table basse signée Ado Chale.

Das Wohnzimmer vereint jeden nur denkbaren Möblierungsstil sowie Deko-Objekte aus verschiedensten Epochen und jedem Winkel der Erde. Auf diesem Bild sieht man einen Lack-Paravent aus dem 18. Jahrhundert hinter einem blauen Satinsofa mit einem Couchtisch von Ado Chale.

El salón reúne cualquier estilo posible de muebles y piezas decorativas de cada periodo y lugar del mundo. Esta imagen muestra un biombo lacado del siglo XVIII tras un sofá de raso azul y una mesa de café de Ado Chale.

Il living come luogo d'incontro di stili d'arredo ed elementi decorativi di ogni epoca e provenienza. Questa prospettiva inquadra un paravento pieghevole del XVIII secolo con finitura in lacca dietro a un divano azzurro in satin con coffee-table di Ado Chale.

The kitchen *was inspired by 1940s American kitchens of some of the most sumptuous mansions in the Hamptons. In the bathroom a Venetian mirror hangs over a black marble sink flanked by red crystal and silver parrot carafes.*

La cuisine *est inspirée des cuisines américaines des années 1940 des plus somptueuses demeures de Hamptons. Dans la salle de bains, le lavabo en marbre noir surplombé d'un miroir vénitien est flanqué de deux carafes perroquets, l'une en cristal rouge et l'autre en argent.*

Das Küchendesign *ist von den amerikanischen Küchen der 1940er Jahre in den luxuriösen Villen der Hamptons inspiriert. Im Badezimmer hängt ein venezianischer Spiegel über einem schwarzen Marmorwaschtisch, auf dem zu beiden Seiten Papageien-Karaffen aus Kristall und Silber stehen.*

La cocina *se inspiró en las cocinas americanas de los años 40 de algunas de las más suntuosas mansiones de Hamptons. En el baño, un espejo veneciano cuelga sobre un lavabo de mármol negro flanqueado por garrafas de plata y cristal rojo con forma de loro.*

La cucina *è ispirata a quelle delle sontuose dimore in voga negli Hamptons americani negli anni '40. Nel bagno, uno specchio veneziano integra un lavabo in marmo nero con brocche a forma di pappagallo in cristallo rosso e argento.*

Spiraling Freedom

Saint-Germain-des-Prés

When interior designer Hubert de Malherbe took on the project of the 19th-century *hôtel particulier*, the curbed shape of its façade brought him back to his childhood travels by train. He was inspired by a sense of movement where bends reconciliate all angles that are never quite straight and spiraling geometric forms close into full circles. The staircase unravels to an open circle in the wall with view of a living room dressed in an array of bright colors against natural tones, furniture from the 1930s to 1960s, and a coffee table, lamps and a rug of his own design. His choice of colors and fabrics are meant to incite the senses—to create a cocoon. An egg-shaped silver-glazed porcelain bathtub sits in a corner of the master bedroom to render homage to his subtle notion of the unexpected. "I am inspired by Warhol; he was playful and dared to question aesthetics and popular culture," says Malherbe. The kitchen in itself is like stepping into a fashionable restaurant with a spectacular bar that shelters cookery intent for *la haute cuisine*.

Lorsque le designer Hubert de Malherbe prend en charge l'aménagement de l'hôtel particulier du XIXe siècle, la façade arrondie lui rappelle les voyages en train sinueux de son enfance. Le sens du mouvement qui l'anime relie par des courbes les angles jamais tout à fait droits et ferme les spirales par des boucles parfaites. Depuis l'escalier, une percée dans le mur donne sur un salon aux teintes vives tranchant sur des tons neutres, avec des meubles des années 1930 à 1960, une table basse, des lampes et de petits tapis créés par l'artiste. Son choix de couleurs et de tissus veut éveiller les sens et créer un cocon. Une baignoire ovale en porcelaine argentée dans un coin de la chambre principale semble illustrer la subtile notion de l'inattendu. « J'ai été inspiré par Warhol, qui adorait jouer et n'a pas hésité à remettre en cause l'esthétique et la culture populaire », précise Malherbe. Dans la cuisine, on croit pénétrer dans un restaurant branché au plan de travail spectaculaire accueillant les « réalisations gastronomiques ».

Als der Innenarchitekt Hubert de Malherbe die Gestaltung der Stadtvilla aus dem 19. Jahrhundert begann, weckte die geschwungene Form der Fassade seine Kindheitserinnerungen an Reisen mit der Eisenbahn. Er ließ sich von dem Gefühl der Bewegung inspirieren, indem gebogene Linien die Winkel, die nie ganz gerade sind, miteinander verbinden und spiralförmig verlaufende, geometrische Formen sich zu ganzen Kreisen schließen. Die Treppe mündet in einem kreisförmigen Durchbruch in der Wand mit Blick auf den Wohnraum, der mit einem Spektrum leuchtender Farben und Naturtönen, Mobiliar aus den 1930er bis 1960er Jahren sowie einem Beistelltisch, Lampen und Teppich nach Malherbes Entwürfen dekoriert ist. Die von ihm getroffene Farb- und Stoffauswahl soll die Sinne anregen und einen Kokon schaffen. Eine silberfarben glasierte Porzellanbadewanne in Eiform steht in einer Ecke des Hauptschlafraumes und huldigt seinem subtilen Sinn für das Unerwartete. „Warhol inspiriert mich, er war verspielt und wagte es, Ästhetik und Pop-Kultur in Frage zu stellen", erklärt Malherbe. Die Küche mit ihrer beeindruckenden Bar, die die Kulisse für Kochausflüge in die Haute Cuisine bildet, vermittelt das Gefühl, ein schickes Restaurant zu betreten.

Cuando el diseñador de interiores Hubert de Malherbe se hizo cargo del proyecto de este *hôtel particulier*, una distinguida casa del siglo XIX, la forma contenida de su fachada lo retrotrajo a los viajes en tren de su infancia. Se inspiró en un sentido del movimiento donde las curvas reconcilian todos los ángulos, nunca del todo rectos, y las formas geométricas en espiral se cierran en círculos completos. La escalera se desenreda en un círculo abierto en la pared, con vistas a un dormitorio vestido con una colección de colores vivos en contraste con tonos naturales, mobiliario de los años 30 a los 60, mesita de café, lámparas y alfombra de diseño propio. Su elección de colores y tejidos está pensada para incitar a los sentidos, para crear un capullo. Una bañera de porcelana con forma de huevo y barnizada en plateado ocupa una esquina del dormitorio principal, como rindiendo homenaje a su sutil noción de lo inesperado. "Mi inspiración es Warhol, él era juguetón y se atrevía a cuestionar la estética y la cultura popular", afirma Malherbe. La cocina en sí misma es como poner los pies en un restaurante de diseño, con un espectacular bar que abriga intenciones culinarias de *la haute cuisine*.

Quando l'architetto d'interni Hubert de Malherbe ha preso in carico il progetto dell'ottocentesco *hôtel particulier*, l'andamento curvilineo della facciata l'ha riportato ai viaggi in treno della sua infanzia. Per questa impresa si è ispirato a un senso del movimento in cui le linee curve risolvono gli angoli mai rigorosamente retti e le forme geometriche spiraleggianti si chiudono in cerchi interi. La scala si dispiega fino a un varco circolare nel muro, aperto su un soggiorno dai colori saturi che emergono sullo sfondo di tinte naturali, tra mobili di epoca compresa tra gli anni '30 e '60 abbinati a tavolino, lampade e tappeto creati da Malherbe. Colori e tessuti sono stati scelti per solleticare i sensi, creare una sorta di guscio. Una vasca ovoidale in porcellana smaltata occupa un angolo della camera padronale, quasi a voler onorare il sottile concetto dell'imprevedibile così caro a Malherbe, il quale afferma: "Mi ispiro a Warhol, perché era giocoso e osava mettere in discussione l'estetica e la cultura popolare". Lo spazio cucina si ispira allo stile di un ristorante alla moda, con un bancone di grande effetto che scherma la zona operativa deputata ad attività di *haute cuisine*.

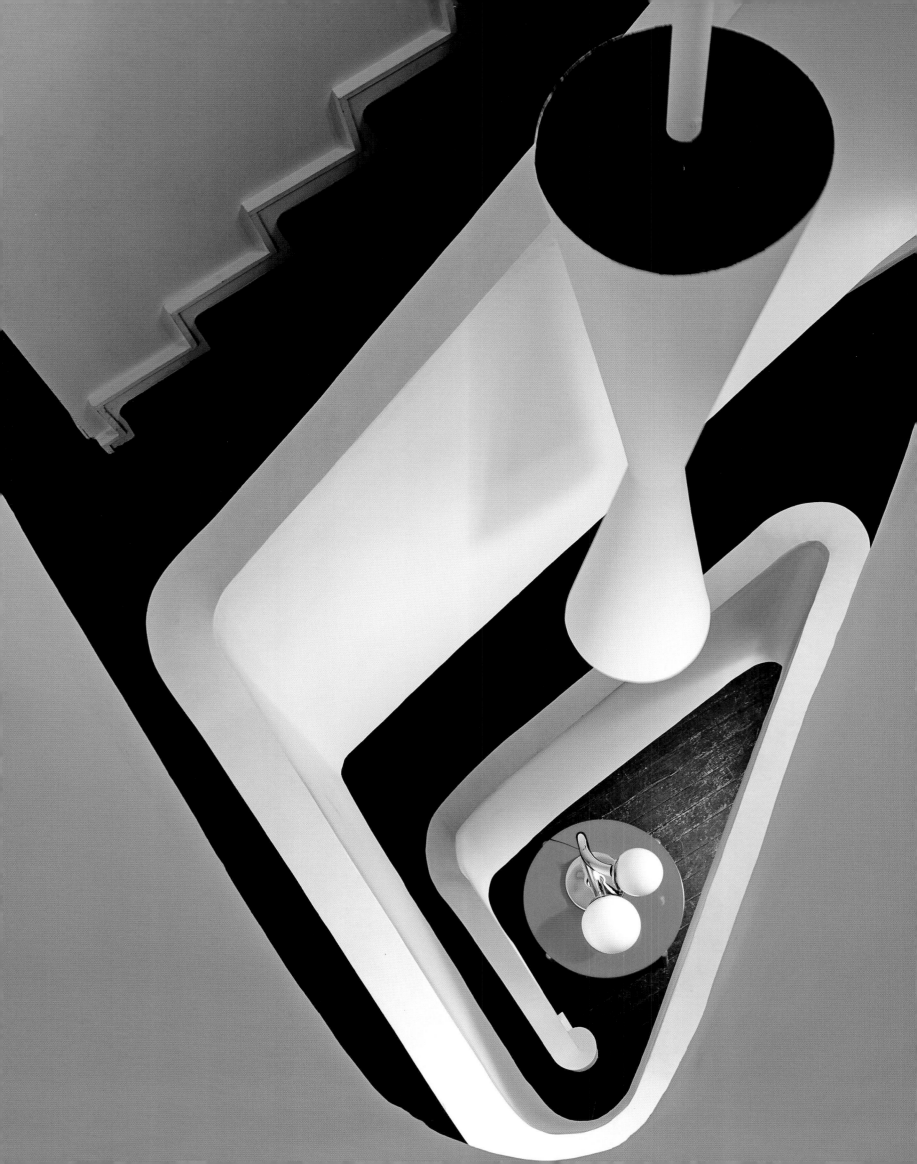

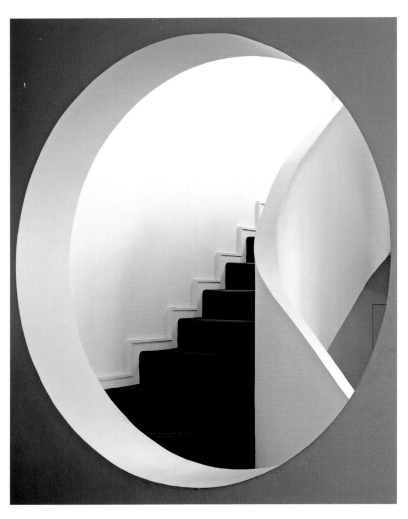

A bistro-fashioned dining area with scarlet red velvet seating and family portraits set the mood for an out of the ordinary day-to-day meal-sharing experience. A Baccarat crystal chandelier and sculpture, designed by Malherbe, and contemporary circular wall sculptures contrast a 17th-century Byzantine statue at the bar.

Avec ses sièges en velours rouge et sa galerie de portraits de famille, ce coin repas style bistrot invite à partager le repas quotidien de manière originale. Le lustre en cristal de Baccarat, la sculpture de Malherbe et les sculptures murales circulaires contemporaines forment un contraste avec la statue byzantine du XVIIe siècle au bar.

Der wie ein Bistro gestaltete Essbereich mit scharlachroten Samtsitzen und Portraits der Familie stimmt auf außergewöhnliche Erlebnisse bei den gemeinsamen täglichen Mahlzeiten ein. Ein Baccarat-Kristallleuchter und eine Skulptur, beide von Malherbe entworfen, sowie zeitgenössische runde Wandskulpturen bilden einen Spannungsbogen zu der byzantinischen Statue aus dem 17. Jahrhundert neben der Bar.

Una zona de almuerzo de estilo bistro, con asientos de terciopelo escarlata y retratos familiares, crea un ambiente que rehúye lo cotidiano en el que compartir las comidas. Araña de luces y escultura de cristal de baccarat, diseñados por Malherbe, y esculturas de pared circulares contemporáneas en contraste con una estatua bizantina del siglo XVII en el bar.

Una zona pranzo stile bistrò, con sedute in velluto rosso scarlatto e ritratti di famiglia, conferisce straordinarietà alla quotidiana esperienza di condivisione del pasto. Il lampadario scultura in cristallo baccarat – disegnato da Malherbe – e le moderne sculture discoidali a parete fanno da contrappunto alla statua bizantina del XVII secolo adiacente al bancone.

Hôtel de Roxie Rocks

Trocadéro

In 2003, recording artist and design visionary Lenny Kravitz founded Kravitz Design Inc. With his design team, they set out on a quest to find a *château* in the middle of Paris. They found a magnificent mansion which became the perfect platform to materialize and showcase his ideas of interior design. Hôtel de Roxie, named after the designer's mother, underwent a few years of renovation before it was fit for the ball. Kravitz decorated the *hôtel particulier* with unique pieces by Kravitz Design, Swarovski crystal chandeliers, polished stainless steel and leather beds, sensually textured rugs and ottomans mixed with vintage European objects by Gabriella Crespi and Joe Colombo along with one of the most complete private collections of 20th-century American studio furniture by Paul Evans.

En 2003, Lenny Kravitz, auteur-compositeur-interprète et designer visionnaire, fonde Kravitz Design Inc. Avec les membres de son équipe, il se met en tête de dénicher un château en plein cœur de Paris. Et il trouve une magnifique demeure qui devient alors la parfaite plateforme pour concrétiser et exposer ses idées en matière d'architecture intérieure. Pour que cette demeure, qu'il baptise Hôtel de Roxie en l'honneur de sa mère, soit à son goût, il fait pendant quelques années exécuter nombre de rénovations. Lenny Kravitz décore ensuite cet hôtel particulier à l'aide d'objets uniques de Kravitz Design, notamment des lustres en cristal Swarovski, des lits en acier inoxydable poli et cuir, des tapis et des ottomanes aux textures sensuelles, le tout mêlé à des meubles européens de collection signés Gabriella Crespi et Joe Colombo. Viennent s'ajouter les pièces de l'une des plus riches collections privées de meubles American Studio du XXe siècle créés par Paul Evans.

2003 gründete der Musiker und Designvisionär Lenny Kravitz das Unternehmen Kravitz Design Inc. und begab sich, zusammen mit seinem Designteam, auf die Suche nach einem Château inmitten von Paris. Sie fanden ein wunderschönes Herrenhaus, das sich perfekt zur Verwirklichung seiner innenarchitektonischen Ideen eignete. Das Hôtel de Roxie, benannt nach der Mutter von Kravitz, wurde mehrere Jahre renoviert, bevor es sich in seiner vollen Pracht zeigte. Kravitz stattete die Stadtvilla mit einzigartigen Stücken von Kravitz Design, Kristalllüstern von Swarovski, glänzenden Edelstahl- und Lederbetten, sinnlich beschaffenen Teppichen und Ottomanen aus und kombinierte sie mit alten Designstücken aus Europa von Gabriella Crespi und Joe Colombo und einer der vollständigsten privaten Sammlungen von Möbeln des 20. Jahrhunderts des Amerikaners Paul Evans.

En el año 2003, el artista musical y visionario del diseño Lenny Kravitz fundó Kravitz Design Inc. Junto a su equipo de diseño, emprendió la búsqueda de un castillo en el centro de París y encontró una opulenta mansión que se convertiría en la plataforma perfecta para materializar y exponer sus ideas sobre el diseño de interiores. El Hôtel de Roxie, así bautizada la mansión por el nombre de la madre del diseñador, fue sometido a reformas durante unos años antes de estar completamente listo. Kravitz decoró este *hôtel particulier* con piezas únicas de Kravitz Design; lámparas de araña de cristal Swarovski, camas de piel y acero inoxidable pulido, alfombras y otomanas de texturas sensuales combinadas con piezas europeas de época de Gabriella Crespi y Joe Colombo, así como con una de las colecciones privadas más completas de mobiliario de estudio americano del siglo XX de Paul Evans.

Nel 2003, il grande produttore discografico e visionario del design Lenny Kravitz fondò la Kravitz Design Inc., e insieme al suo nuovo team di artisti partì alla ricerca di uno chateau nel cuore di Parigi. La scelta cadde su un maestoso palazzo che divenne la cornice ideale per la realizzazione e l'esposizione delle ammirevoli idee di Kravitz in fatto di design degli interni. Per qualche anno l'Hôtel de Roxie, che porta il nome della madre di chi lo progettò, fu sottoposto a un'opera di ristrutturazione che gli diede nuovo lustro in vista dell'ambizioso ruolo che avrebbe rivestito. Kravitz ne curò minuziosamente gli interni, inserendovi pezzi unici firmati Kravitz Design, lampadari di cristallo Swarovski, letti in pelle e acciaio inossidabile lucidato, tappeti di voluttuosa fattura e ottomani frapposti a oggetti d'epoca di provenienza europea realizzati da Gabriella Crespi e Joe Colombo, il tutto corredato da una delle collezioni private tra le più complete al mondo di mobili da studio americani Paul Evans del XX secolo.

The Petit Salon *displays Baccarat chandelier and candelabras, a sexy sofa by Kravitz Design and a coffee table by Armand Jonckers. The dining room table and chairs are designed by Karl Springer and flanked by Baccarat candelabras, wall sconces and chandelier; the African statues and background mirror come together with a shag carpet creation by Shagtastic.*

Au petit salon, *on peut surtout admirer le lustre et les candélabres en cristal de Baccarat, mais aussi un canapé chic de Kravitz Design et une table basse d'Armand Jonckers. Signées Karl Springer, la table et les chaises noires de la salle à manger sont mises en valeur par les candélabres, les appliques murales et le lustre en cristal de Baccarat. Les statues africaines et le miroir à l'arrière-plan s'accordent parfaitement avec le tapis Shagtastic.*

Der Petit Salon *weist einen Baccarat-Lüster und Kronleuchter auf, ein sexy Sofa von Kravitz Design und einen Couchtisch von Armand Jonckers. Tisch und Stühle des Esszimmers von Karl Springer werden von Baccarat-Kronleuchtern, -Wandleuchtern und -Lüstern eingerahmt. Afrikanische Statuen und ein Spiegel im Hintergrund runden den Raum gemeinsam mit einer Zottelteppichkreation von Shagtastic ab.*

El Petite Salon *presenta una lámpara de araña y candelabros Baccarat, sofá sexy de Kravitz Design y mesa de café de Armand Jonckers. La mesa y las sillas del comedor, diseñadas por Karl Springer y flanqueadas por candelabros, apliques y lámpara de araña Baccarat, estatuas africanas y un espejo en segundo plano, forman un conjunto sobre una alfombra de pelo largo, creación de Shagtastic.*

Nel Petit Salon *convivono un lampadario e candelabri Baccarat, un sofà Kravitz Design dalle linee seducenti e un coffee-table di Armand Jonckers. Nella sala da pranzo, il tavolo e le sedie disegnati da Karl Springer, i candelabri Baccarat, i portalampade a muro e il lampadario, le statue africane e lo specchio in secondo piano formano un tutt'uno con il tappeto a pelo lungo creato da Shagtastic.*

The view of the master bathroom displays a rectangular block bathtub and floors in Noir Saint Laurent marble, a painting by Tatiana Podmarkova (Madonnas) in the background and Baccarat candelabras, wall sconces and chandelier. The magnificent Gilt Hand Foot chair sculpture by Pedro Friedeberg stands against the wall with a prototype Table Gun lamp by Philippe Starck at its side.

Dans la salle de bains principale, une baignoire rectangulaire en marbre Noir Saint Laurent est posée sur un sol, lui-aussi en marbre Saint Laurent. Une peinture des « Madonnas » de Tatiana Podmarkova ainsi que des candélabres, des appliques murales et des lustres, tous en cristal de Baccarat, décorent la pièce. Le prototype de la lampe « Table Gun » conçue par Philippe Starck éclaire la magnifique chaise-objet dorée « Gilt Hand Foot » de Pedro Friedeberg qui est adossée au mur.

Im Hauptbadezimmer befinden sich eine rechteckige Badewanne und Boden aus Noir Saint Laurent-Marmor, das Gemälde „Madonnas" von Tatiana Podmarkova im Hintergrund, sowie Baccarat-Kandelaber, -Wandleuchten und -Kronleuchter. Die prächtige Stuhlskulptur „Gilt Hand Foot" von Pedro Friedeberg steht mit dem Rücken zur Wand an der Seite eines Prototypen der „Table Gun"-Lampe von Philippe Starck.

Esta vista del cuarto de baño principal muestra una bañera rectangular y suelos de mármol Noir Saint Laurent, el cuadro "Madonnas" de Tatiana Podmarkova en segundo plano y candelabros, apliques de pared y lámparas de araña Baccarat. La magnífica silla escultura "Gilt Hand Foot" de Pedro Friedeberg se encuentra frente a la pared, acompañada de un propotipo de lámpara "Table Gun" de Philippe Starck situado a su lado.

La vista sul bagno principale illustra una vasca e pavimenti in marmo Noir Saint Laurent, il quadro "Madonnas" di Tatiana Podmarkova fa da retroscena e spiccano candelabri, applique e lampadari Baccarat. La magnifica scultura raffigurante una sedia intitolata "Gilt Hand Foot" di Pedro Friedeberg volta le spalle alla parete ed è accompagnata da un prototipo di lampada "Table Gun" di Philippe Starck posta sul suo fianco.

Reto Guntli and Caroline Sarkozy, Photo: Agi Simoes

Caroline Sarkozy, Editor

As an interior designer, Caroline Sarkozy travels all around the world. She decorates the very private interiors of international clients to which she brings luxury, comfort and French elegance. Sarkozy, through her eclectic and never ending curiosity, creates for her clients unique collections of objects and furniture. From a nomadic childhood, in the footsteps of a diplomatic stepfather, Caroline has aquired an accute taste for travel. She succeeds in combining charm and thoroughness, giving authenticity and personality to the homes she decorates. She dares to mix styles, textures and colors. With her degree from Parsons School of Design in New York City, her collaboration with Andrée Putman has given her recognition. Creating her own studio in 1998, CS décoration in Paris, Sarkozy handles international projects, mixing her original creations with detailled and elegant interior design schemes.

L'architecte d'intérieur et décoratrice, Caroline Sarkozy, parcourt le globe pour décorer les intérieurs très privés d'une clientèle internationale à laquelle elle apporte luxe, raffinement à la française et collection d'objets d'art. D'une enfance nomade, suivant un beau-père diplomate, Caroline a un goût prononcé pour les voyages. Il en découle un style audacieux, alliant charme et rigueur, qui donne des racines à chaque lieu qu'elle décore. Elle ose mélanger les styles, les époques, les matières et les couleurs. Sa formation auprès d'Andrée Putman et son diplôme américain de la Parsons School of Design de New York lui ont donné un savoir-faire reconnu. Avec la création en 1998 de l'agence CS décoration à Paris, Caroline prend en charge en globalité des projets d'aménagement d'intérieur et de décoration, dans lesquels elle associe ses créations originales à une conception détaillée et élégante de l'architecture d'intérieur.

Die Innenarchitektin Caroline Sarkozy reist um die ganze Welt, um die privaten Residenzen ihrer internationalen Kunden einzurichten und sie mit Luxuriösem, französischer Finesse und Kunstobjekten auszustatten. Als Kind führte sie im Gefolge ihres Diplomatenstiefvaters ein Nomadendasein und hat daher heute ein Faible für das Reisen. Daraus entspringt ihr mutiger Stil, der Klassisches mit Charme vereint und jedem Haus und jeder Wohnung Authentizität und Persönlichkeit verleiht. Sie wagt es, Stile, Epochen, Materialien und Farben zu mischen. Durch ihre Ausbildung bei Andrée Putman und den Besuch der New Yorker Parsons School of Design verfügt sie über anerkannte Kenntnisse. Seit sie 1998 die Agentur CS décoration in Paris ins Leben rief, übernimmt sie internationale Projekte, für die sie ihre eigenen Kreationen mit einer detaillierten und eleganten Konzeption der Inneneinrichtung verknüpft.

La arquitecta de interiores y diseñadora Caroline Sarkozy recorre el mundo para decorar los interiores más íntimos de una clientela internacional a la que deleita con lujo, refinamiento francés y colecciones de piezas de arte. Caroline tuvo una infancia nómada y, siguiendo los pasos de un padrastro diplomático, siente una gran pasión por los viajes. De ellos nace su estilo audaz, que combina encanto y rigor y deja su rastro en cada lugar que decora. Se atreve con la mezcla de estilos, épocas, materias y colores. Su formación con Andrée Putman y sus estudios en la Parsons School of Design de Nueva York le han permitido desarrollar una reconocida maestría. Con la creación de la agencia CS décoration en París en 1998, Caroline se hace cargo de forma global de proyectos de diseño de interiores y decoración, en los que combina sus originales creaciones con una concepción detallada y elegante de la arquitectura de interiores.

Architetto e décoratrice d'interni, Caroline Sarkozy viaggia da un capo all'altro del mondo per arredare gli spazi privati di una clientela internazionale rivestendoli di un'eleganza tutta francese, fatta di lusso, comfort e raffinatezza. Animata da una curiosità a tutto tondo che pare non avere confini, crea collezioni di oggetti d'arte ed elementi d'arredo senza pari. Caroline, che ha trascorso un'infanzia nomade al seguito del patrigno diplomatico, possiede una spiccata passione per i viaggi, da cui ha tratto uno stile audace in cui il fascino si mescola al rigore, in una magica alchimia decorativa che dona autenticità e carattere ad ogni casa che porta la sua firma. Ama mescolare gli stili, le epoche, i materiali e i colori. La collaborazione con Andrée Putman e il diploma conseguito alla Parsons School of Design di New York le hanno conferito statura internazionale. Dal 1998, anno in cui fonda l'agenzia CS décoration di Parigi, Caroline prende in carico progetti globali di progettazione e decorazione d'interni, in cui associa le proprie creazioni originali a un concetto dettagliato ed elegante di interior design.

Reto Guntli, Photographer

Swiss photographer Reto Guntli travels to all continents reporting on architecture, interiors, people, art, design, travel, and gardens. Having photographed and produced 30 coffee table books for the largest publishing houses in the world, his watchful eye on international cities and their lifestyles is known all over. He regularly contributes to dozens of the most prestigious international magazines such as *Architectural Digest, Vogue, Elle Decor, Condé Nast Traveler, Hotel & Lodges, Geo,* and many others. Reto Guntli is also known for his advertising shoots for international hotels and has published several books on the best hotels, resorts and spas around the globe. He is based in Zurich, Switzerland and is represented by zapaimages (www.zapaimages.com).

Le photographe suisse Reto Guntli voyage sur tous les continents pour faire des reportages sur l'architecture, les intérieurs, les gens, l'art, le design, les voyages et les jardins. Il a participé à la production de 30 ouvrages illustrés pour les plus grandes maisons d'édition du monde. Son œil averti sur les villes internationales et leur art de vivre est connu partout. Il contribue régulièrement à une douzaine de magazines internationaux prestigieux, parmi lesquels *Architectural Digest*, *Vogue*, *Elle Decor*, *Condé Nast Traveler* et *Geo*. Réputé pour les prises de vue publicitaires qu'il a réalisées pour les hôtels internationaux, Reto Guntli a également publié plusieurs ouvrages sur les meilleurs hôtels, resorts et spas de la planète. Établi à Zurich, il est représenté par zapaimages (www.zapaimages.com).

Der Schweizer Fotograf Reto Guntli bereist alle Kontinente und berichtet über Architektur, Inneneinrichtung, Menschen, Kunst, Design, Reisen und Gärten. Für die größten Verlage der Welt hat er seine Aufnahmen in 30 Bildbänden veröffentlicht. Sein wachsames Auge, das auf internationale Städte und deren Lebensstil gerichtet ist, ist somit überall bekannt. In Dutzenden der angesehensten internationalen Zeitschriften wie *Architectural Digest, Vogue, Elle Decor, Condé Nast Traveler, Hotel & Lodges, Geo* und viele andere werden seine Beiträge regelmäßig veröffentlicht. Darüber hinaus ist Reto Guntli für seine Werbeaufnahmen für internationale Hotels bekannt. Er hat auch mehrere Bücher über die besten Hotels, Resorts und Spas rund um die Welt veröffentlicht. Er ist in Zürich beheimatet und wird von zapaimages (www.zapaimages.com) vertreten.

El fotógrafo suizo Reto Guntli viaja por todos los continentes haciendo notas sobre arquitectura, interiorismo, gente, arte, diseño, viajes y jardines. Luego de haber participado en la fotografía y en la producción de 30 libros ilustrados de gran tamaño para las más grandes editoriales del mundo, su conocimiento de las ciudades internacionales y de sus estilos de vida es públicamente reconocido. Es un colaborador frecuente de decenas de las más prestigiosas revistas internacionales tales como *Architectural Digest, Vogue, Elle Decor, Condé Nast Traveler, Hotel & Lodges, Geo* y muchas otras. A Reto Guntli también se lo conoce por sus fotografías publicitarias para hoteles internacionales y ha publicado varios libros sobre los mejores hoteles, resorts y spas en todo el mundo. Reside en Zurich, Suiza y lo representa zapaimages (www.zapaimages.com).

Il fotografo svizzero Reto Guntli viaggia in tutto il mondo facendo servizi su architettura, interni, persone, arte, design, viaggi e giardini. Avendo prodotto 30 libri di fotografie da lui scattate per le più importanti case editrici del mondo, il suo occhio attento alle città internazionali e al loro stile di vita è noto a tutti. Contribuisce regolarmente a decine di prestigiose riviste internazionali quali *Architectural Digest, Vogue, Elle Decor, Condé Nast Traveler, Hotel & Lodges, Geo* e molte altre. Reto Guntli è anche famoso per i suoi servizi pubblicitari per alberghi internazionali ed ha pubblicato diversi libri sui migliori alberghi, centri di villeggiatura e centri benessere del mondo. Vive a Zurigo, in Svizzera, ed è rappresentato da zapaimages (www.zapaimages.com).

www.retoguntli.com

Debra Derieux Matos, Photo: © ArtMan

Debra Derieux Matos, Writer

Debra Derieux Matos has come a long way from her native Puerto Rico. As a broadcast journalist, she began her career in Chicago with a radio program called *De Todo Un Poco*, then went to New York City where she worked as a producer and reporter for several TV networks while completing a postgraduate degree in Latin American Literature at New York University. New York took her to Paris—via London—where she produced the coverage of the World Cup 1998 for a US TV network and stayed on as a correspondent. Today, as she enjoys life in Paris with her daughters and a wonderful network of friends from all over the globe, she continues freelancing for radio and TV and writing pieces on fashion and lifestyle for international publications.

Debra Derieux Matos a accompli un long périple depuis son Porto Rico natal. Journaliste de radio et de télévision, elle commence sa carrière à Chicago avec une émission de radio intitulée *De Todo Un Poco*, puis elle part pour New York où elle travaille comme productrice et reportrice pour plusieurs chaînes de télévision tout en faisant des études de littérature latino-américaine à l'université de New York (NYU). Elle passe ensuite par Londres pour arriver à Paris, où elle couvre la Coupe du monde de football de 1998 pour une chaîne américaine, qui l'engage comme correspondante. Aujourd'hui, elle est heureuse de vivre à Paris, entourée de ses filles et d'un réseau d'amis très cosmopolite. Elle poursuit son activité pour la radio et la télévision, tout en écrivant des articles sur la mode et l'art de vivre dans des publications internationales.

Seit dem Verlassen ihrer Heimat Puerto Rico hat Debra Derieux Matos einen langen Weg hinter sich gebracht. Ihre Karriere begann in Chicago als Hörfunkjournalistin mit einer Radiosendung, die sich *De Todo Un Poco* nannte. Danach ging sie nach New York, wo sie für verschiedene Fernsehsender als Produzentin und Journalistin arbeitete und zusätzlich noch in ihrem Studienfach, Lateinamerikanische Literatur, an der NYU promovierte. Über London kam sie nach Paris, wo sie für einen amerikanischen Fernsehsender für die Berichterstattung zur Fußballweltmeisterschaft 1998 verantwortlich war und danach als Korrespondentin blieb. In Paris lebt sie auch heute noch mit ihren Töchtern und einem wunderbaren Kreis an Freuden aus der gesamten Welt. Sie arbeitet weiterhin als freie Journalistin für Radio und Fernsehen und schreibt für internationale Publikationen Artikel zu Mode und Lifestyle.

Debra Derieux Matos ha recorrido un largo camino desde su Puerto Rico natal. Inició su carrera como periodista de radio y televisión en Chicago con un programa llamado De todo un poco, para luego dirigirse a Nueva York, donde trabajó como reportera productora para diversas cadenas de televisión mientras realizaba estudios de posgrado en literatura latinoamericana en la NYU. Posteriormente, Nueva York la conduciría a París —haciendo escala en Londres— donde realizó la cobertura informativa de la Copa Mundial de 1998 para una cadena de televisión estadounidense y donde se quedó a trabajar como corresponsal. Actualmente disfruta de su vida en París en compañía de sus hijas y una espléndida red de amigos de todos los rincones del mundo, mientras sigue trabajando por cuenta propia para la radio y la televisión. Asimismo, escribe artículos sobre moda y estilo de vida para publicaciones internacionales.

Debra Derieux Matos ha fatto parecchia strada da quando ha spiccato il volo dalla nativa Puerto Rico. Come giornalista radiotelevisiva ha iniziato la sua carriera a Chicago alla guida di un programma radiofonico intitolato *De Todo Un Poco*, poi si è trasferita a New York, dove ha lavorato come capo reporter per diversi network televisivi frequentando contemporaneamente un corso post-laurea in letteratura latinoamericana alla NYU. Dalla Grande Mela, passando per Londra, è approdata a Parigi; qui ha diretto la copertura della World Cup 1998 per un network televisivo statunitense e ha scelto di continuare nella capitale francese la sua carriera di corrispondente. Oggi, mentre si gode la vita parigina insieme alle figlie e a uno splendido entourage di amici provenienti da ogni angolo del mondo, prosegue la sua attività di giornalista freelance per la radio e la televisione e scrive articoli di moda e lifestyle per testate internazionali.

Agi Simoes, Photo: Reto Guntli

Agi Simoes, Photographer

Brazilian photographer Agi Simoes is based in Zurich, Switzerland and is an international photographer of interiors, architecture and portraiture for magazines such as *Casa Vogue, Architectural Digest, Elle Decor,* and many others. He has also published lifestyle books on Rio de Janeiro, artists in Brazil, Buenos Aires, and Majorca. He often travels and collaborates with Reto Guntli on extensive book and reportage projects.

Photographe brésilien de renommée internationale, Agi Simoes est établi à Zurich, en Suisse. Il photographie des intérieurs, des extérieurs et des portraits pour de nombreux magazines, parmi lesquels *Casa Vogue, Architectural Digest* et *Elle Decor.* Il a également publié des ouvrages sur l'art de vivre à Rio de Janeiro, ainsi que sur des artistes du Brésil, de Buenos Aires et de Majorque. Il voyage souvent et collabore avec Reto Guntli sur d'importants projets de livres et de reportages.

Der brasilianische Fotograf Agi Simoes hat sein Lager in Zürich aufgeschlagen. Er fotografiert Inneneinrichtung, Architektur und Portraits für Zeitschriften wie *Casa Vogue, Architectural Digest, Elle Decor* und viele andere. Außerdem hat er Bücher über den Lebensstil in Rio de Janeiro, Künstler in Brasilien, Buenos Aires und Mallorca veröffentlicht. Er reist oft mit Reto Guntli und arbeitet mit ihm an umfangreichen Buch- und Reportageprojekten zusammen.

El fotógrafo brasileño Agi Simoes está radicado en Zurich, Suiza y es un fotógrafo internacional de interiores, arquitectura y retratos para revistas como *Casa Vogue, Architectural Digest, Elle Decor* y muchas otras. También publicó libros sobre el estilo de vida en Río de Janeiro, Buenos Aires y Mallorca. Suele viajar y colaborar con Reto Guntli en grandes proyectos de libros y reportajes.

Il fotografo brasiliano Agi Simoes vive a Zurigo, in Svizzera, ed è un fotografo di interni, di architettura e di ritrattistica di fama internazionale. Collabora con riviste come *Casa Vogue, Architectural Digest, Elle Decor* e molte altre. Ha anche pubblicato libri di stile di vita su Rio de Janeiro e su artisti brasiliani, di Buenos Aires e di Majorca. Viaggia spesso e collabora con Reto Guntli per libri e reportage di ampio respiro.

© 2010 teNeues Verlag GmbH + Co. KG, Kempen

Photographs © 2010 Reto Guntli
All photographs courtesy of zapaimages (www.zapaimages.com)
All rights reserved.

Edited by Caroline Sarkozy
Text written by Debra Derieux Matos
Proofreading by Maria Regina Madarang
French translation by Claude Checconi, proofreading by Sabine Boccador
German translation by Haike Falkenberg, Irene Eisenhut
Spanish and Italian translations by RR Communications, Romina Russo
Design by Silke Braun
Color separation by Medien Team-Vreden

Published by teNeues Publishing Group

teNeues Verlag GmbH + Co. KG
Am Selder 37, 47906 Kempen, Germany
Phone: 0049-2152-916-0
Fax: 0049-2152-916-111
e-mail: books@teneues.de

Press department: Andrea Rehn
Phone: 0049-2152-916-202
e-mail: arehn@teneues.de

teNeues Publishing Company
7 West 18th Street, New York, NY 10011, USA
Phone: 001-212-627-9090
Fax: 001-212-627-9511

teNeues Publishing UK Ltd.
21 Marlowe Court, Lymer Avenue, London SE19 1LP, Great Britain
Phone: 0044-208-670-7522
Fax: 0044-208-670-7523

teNeues France S.A.R.L.
39, rue des Billets, 18250 Henrichemont, France
Phone: 0033-2-4826-9348
Fax: 0033-1-7072-3482

www.teneues.com

ISBN 978-3-8327-9371-5

Printed in Italy

Bibliographic information published by the Deutsche Nationalbibliothek.
The Deutsche Nationalbibliothek lists this publication in the Deutsche Nationalbibliografie;
detailed bibliographic data are available in the Internet at http://dnb.d-nb.de.

teNeues Publishing Group
Kempen
Cologne
Düsseldorf
Hamburg
London
Munich
New York
Paris

teNeues